THE COMPLETE BOOK OF
TEDDY BEAR
MAKING TECHNIQUES

THE COMPLETE BOOK OF
TEDDY BEAR
MAKING TECHNIQUES

Alicia Merrett and Ann Stephens

RUNNING PRESS
PHILADELPHIA · LONDON

A QUARTO BOOK

Copyright © 1998 Quarto Inc.

9 8 7 6 5 4 3 2 1

ISBN 0-7624-0349-7

Library of Congress Cataloging-in-Publication Number
98-65181

This book was designed and produced by
Quarto Publishing plc
The Old Brewery
6 Blundell Street
London N7 9BH

Editors Judith Evans, Ulla Weinberg
Art Editor/Designer Julie Francis
Copy Editor Leslie Viney
Photographers Martin Norris, Les Wies, Paul Forrester
Illustrations Elsa Godfrey
Picture Researcher Zoë Holtermann
Editorial Director Pippa Rubinstein
Art Director Moira Clinch

Typeset by Central Southern Typesetters, Eastbourne
Manufactured in Singapore by United Graphics (Pte) Ltd
Printed in China by Leefung-Asco Printers Ltd

This book may be ordered by mail from the publisher.
Please include $2.50 for postage and handling.
But try your bookstore first!

Running Press Publishers
125 South Twenty-second Street
Philadelphia, Pennsylvania 19103–4399

Contents

Introduction   6
Safety   8
Tools and Equipment   10
Materials   14
Stitches   19

BEAR MAKING TECHNIQUES   **20**
Teddy Bear Design   22
Patterns   28
Fabric Layout, Marking, and Cutting   30
Stitching the Bear   33
Stitching the Head   36

ASSEMBLING THE BEAR   **44**
Putting Joints in the Bear   46
Turning and Putting Joints In   52
Stuffing the Bear   58

TEDDY BEAR FEATURES   **64**
Eyes   66
Noses   72
Mouths   78
Ears   80
Finishing Bears   82
Antiquing or Distressing   86

MINIATURE BEARS   **90**

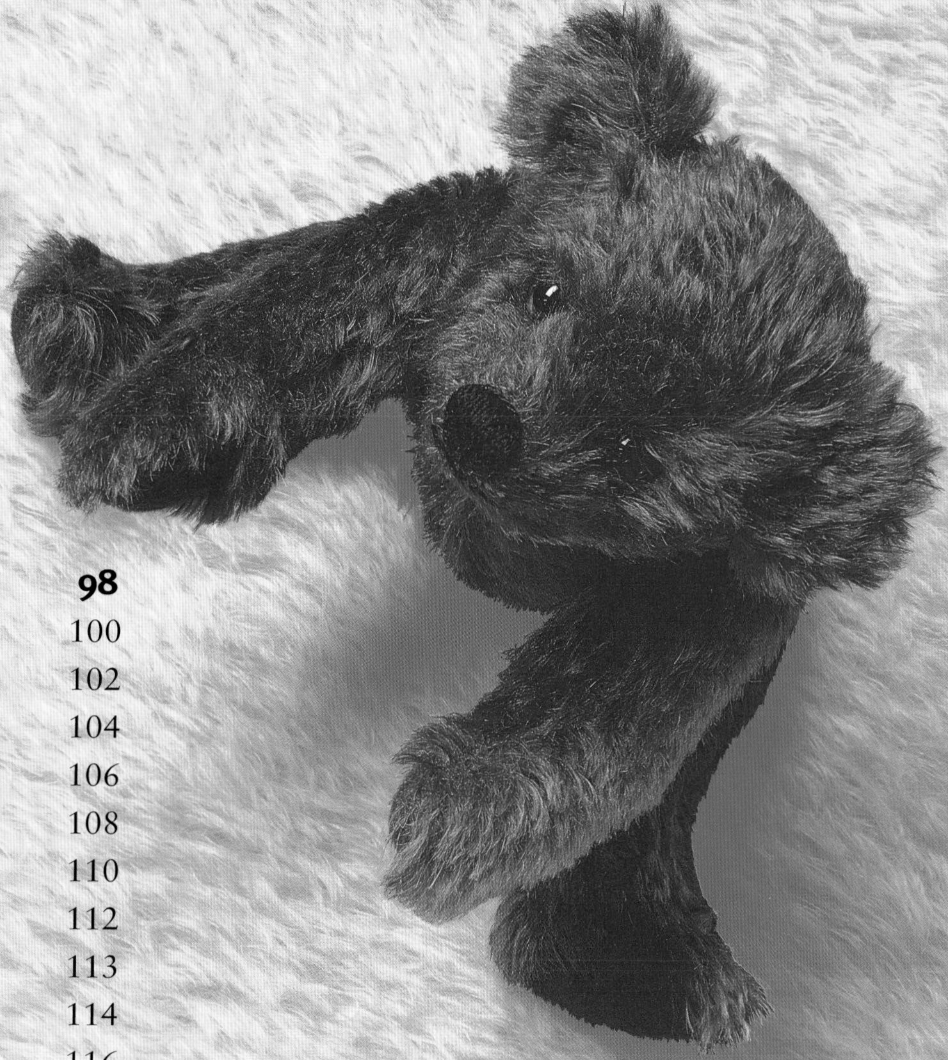

MAKING GARMENTS 98

Making Clothes for Bears 100

Vest and Bow Tie 102

Collars and Ties 104

Hats 106

Skirt 108

Dress 110

Pants 112

Tracksuit 113

Dungarees 114

Shirt 116

GALLERY 118

Traditional Bears 120

Classic Bears 122

Evolution of the Classic Bear 126

Bears on All Fours 128

Special Features 130

Simple Clothes 132

Unusual Costumes 134

Homey Bears 136

Pairs of Bears 138

Scenes 140

Fantasy Bears 142

Special Bears 144

Miniature Bears 146

Patterns - Mix and Match 148

Index 158

Credits 160

Introduction

The traditional jointed Teddy Bear was born in 1903; whether it was in Germany or in America is still a matter of controversy. It soon took hold of people's imaginations throughout the world, and became a favorite toy and companion.

Those early Teddies have become expensive antiques, much sought after by collectors. Because they are rare but so desirable, people began to make their own modern bears to look like the traditional ones. Soon many variations appeared, and the current crop of artists' bears is available in many different styles.

WHERE TO START Making your own bear is not difficult; if you can do some basic sewing, this book will show you the rest. There is nothing more rewarding than making your first fully jointed traditional Teddy Bear. All your worries disappear when you become absorbed in creating these special little characters. In addition, what can start out as an enjoyable hobby can grow into a thriving and totally rewarding business, as the Gallery photographs of some of our top artists illustrate.

With the overwhelming choice of fabrics, components, patterns, and advice available nowadays, it is often quite difficult to know where to start. The idea of this book is to give you a sound foundation on which to build. Once you have mastered the basics, there is no limit to what you may achieve.

TECHNIQUES There are as many ways to make bears as there are artists. We can show you our way which has been tried and tested, not only through making bears but also through teaching workshops. We try to address the questions that most people ask when they begin bearmaking, plus giving details of several more specialized techniques to start you on your way to creating really original bears. The more bears you make the more your skills will improve, and the more you will like to experiment with new ideas that will make your bears stand out from the rest and have that extra touch of magic that makes the difference between a bear maker and a true Bear Artist.

◀ Original antique bear, made by the German firm of Steiff around 1920.

▼ Traditional bear featuring long curved arms and pointed muzzle. Designed by Ann Stephens.

This book is designed for you to dip into when doing a particular procedure, but if you are a novice at bearmaking then it will take you through the process in detail from design to finishing off. At the end of the book there is a set of "mix-and-match" patterns provided for you to try out all of the techniques.

The most important thing to remember is that creating bears is fun; but be warned, it is also totally addictive! **Happy Bearmaking.**

Alicia Merrett and Ann Stephens

▲ Miniature replica of a 1903 German bear, made by Iris and Ches Chesney.

◀ Modern bear by Diana Oldacre, fully dressed for bedtime, carrying his own small calico bear, made by Alicia Merrett.

▲ Contemporary collector's bear by Diana Oldacre, designed to slump like a much loved older one.

▲ Modern artist bear with special joints by Sue Tolcher.

Safety

When making bears you have to be aware of certain safety requirements, but this must not deter you from making bears for other people, either as gifts or for sale. If the requirements are understood and adhered to, then it is a simple process that will ensure both your protection and that of the recipient.

There are two distinct types of bear that will be referred to throughout the book. The first is known as a Collectors' Bear and the second as a Child Safe Bear. These terms are self-evident, but it is important to identify which category your bear falls into before giving it to someone else.

COMPONENTS Every component used will be in one category or the other. It is clearly stated in each section which is which, but here is a quick reference key for you to refer to. It depends on the components used whether the bear is considered as child safe or not.

COLLECTORS' BEARS

These bears are usually made in the traditional way with traditional materials. In the days of the first bears there were no such things as man-made fibers, so natural fillings and fabrics were used. This of course meant that they presented a high fire risk. In addition, the components were made out of metal pins and fiber board disks; the eyes were glass and put in with twisted wire.

Many artists still use these components today, but with the introduction of Trading Safety Standards in the early sixties, they are not allowed to sell them for children, a child in this case being anyone under the age of 14 years. Labeling on these bears must carry the words "collectors' item only" and "unsuitable for children under 14." Other information must include a full list of components used plus the maker's contact name and address. It is not necessary to write your full address, just the zip code and town will suffice.

◀ A collector's bear by Carol-Lynn Rössel Waugh, fitted with metal-based joints and traditional glass eyes.

◀ A child safe mohair bear made by Hilary Clark, with polyester stuffing and plastic safety eyes and joints.

CHILD SAFE BEARS

It would be a great pity if all bears were made for the adult collectors' market only. Children still love bears and should be given the opportunity to grow up with a loving dependable companion. There is a distinct difference between toy bears and traditional bears. It is possible to make bears that look every bit the collectors' item, but still comply with the safety requirements. The labeling must be clear and again list all of the components as for collectors' bears. All components used in the making of these bears must also comply to high standards. Each material and component supplier will be able to produce documentation to this effect. By the same token the artists should also keep documentation about each bear on file, including patterns, samples of fabrics, and notes on which components were used. These will all be necessary should the Trading Standards Office need the information.

Labels, although mainly used for information, may also be used to enhance the look of your bears. There are many different ways of labeling, with sewn or swing tag. Remember that if you are eventually selling your bears, then each label will be a miniature advertisement. If not, it is a stylish way of keeping a record of your bears and when they were made.

COMPLIANCE OF MATERIALS

As a general rule, the components listed in the left hand column should be suitable for children's bears. Those on the right hand column should usually only be used in collectors' bears. There are exceptions, however. If you are making children's bears, you should always get written confirmation of the suitability of components from your suppliers.

CHILDREN'S BEARS

- Polyester filling
- Pellets (if put in a bag)
- Kapok

- Black or white plastic joints

- Plastic safety eyes and noses
- Mohair
- Wool felt

- Suede
- Growlers
- Embroidery thread for noses

COLLECTORS' BEARS

- Wood wool
- Pellets, loose

- Cotter pin joints
- Nut and bolt joints

- Glass eyes

- Spectacles
- Musical movements
- Bells

Tools and Equipment

We have compiled a list of the basic items needed to set up a well-equipped tool box. You may think that some are a luxury until you actually use them and discover the advantage of having just the right tools for the job.

It is often said that a bad craftsman blames his tools. But if you have the right tools for the job, then the chances of being a bad craftsman are much fewer. In order to do a job well it makes sense to spend a little time and money putting together a useful and comprehensive tool kit. If you will be spending large amounts of money on top quality fabrics and components over the years, then it would be a shame to spoil your bears by using inferior tools.

SEWING MATERIALS Sewing materials are also part of the tools of the trade, as bears require special needles, thread, and scissors to achieve a good result, so you should look at your sewing box and complete it with the special items required.

NEEDLES

1 Fine small milliners' or quilters' needles for miniature bearmaking.

2 Sharps, for normal size bear sewing.

3 Embroidery crewel needles, with a larger eye, for thicker threads. These can also be used for soft sculpting.

4 Long thin darners, for embroidering noses in small bears.

5 Long thicker darners, for embroidering noses in medium and large bears.

6 3½in needle for embroidering noses and fixing eyes in smaller bears.

7 Curved needle for attaching ears.

8 Extra-long 7in needle for fixing eyes in medium and larger bears.

9 Leather needle, with three-faceted point, for easier piercing

10 Needle puller.

PINS

11 Colored-headed pins, to be easily identified in long pile fabrics.

12 T-shaped pins, for holding ears in place.

SEWING THREADS

13 Cotton/polyester thread, for normal sewing.

14 Hand-quilting thread, slightly thicker and stronger.

15 Invisible thread (nylon monofilament) for stitching miniature bears.

16 Strong nylon thread for attaching eyes and ears.

EMBROIDERY THREADS

17 Perle cotton—No. 5 for small and medium bears.

18 Perle cotton—No. 3 (thicker) for larger bears.

19 Stranded cotton—for miniature bears.

20 Fantasy embroidery thread for unusual bears.

SPECIALISED TOOLS

The special tools recommended for making teddies are easily available from many bear making suppliers. In some cases they can be substituted by similar tools found around the house, but those are not likely to give the same results.

1 Small sharp pointed scissors for cutting bearmaking fabrics.

2 Scalpel, as an alternative cutting tool for fur fabrics.

3 Long nose pliers for turning cotter pin jonts and forming the loop on wired glass eyes.

4 Cotter key, an alternative tool for turning cotter pin joints, available in large and small.

5 Forceps (also called hemostats) for turning narrow pieces and filling awkward corners.

6 Joint punch for tightening plastic safety joints.

7 Nut driver for turning nut and bolt joints. Two are needed per joint, and they come in different sizes for different bolts, in small, medium, and large.

8 Ratchet wrench— alternative tool for turning nut and bolt joints. A pair of pliers, preferably self-locking, is also neded to hold the other end of the bolt.

9 Wooden stuffing stick for polyester and Kapok, with two blunt rounded ends, especially designed to avoid it poking through the fabric.

10 Metal stuffing stick with v-notched end, for wood wool.

11 Awl, for making holes in the fabric by separating threads instead of cutting through them.

12 Marking tools: pencil, blue ball-point pen, and white correcting pen for dark fabrics.

13 Teasel Brush, a small stiff wire brush, especially designed for mohair fabrics.

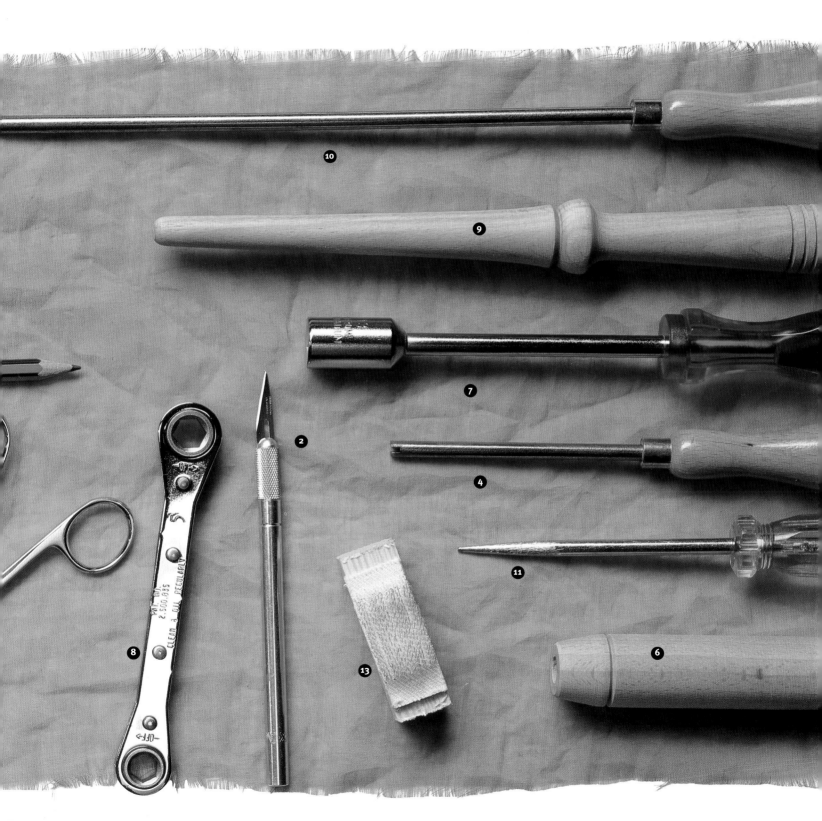

Materials

The early bears were sewn from plush fabrics made from mohair. The selection of modern fabrics, some imitating the antique ones, others with a different feel and touch, is amazingly large and attractive.

Choose your fabric with care. There are many options: mohairs with shorter and longer fibers; with dense or sparse hairs; with straight, wavy, distressed, feathery, or bouclé type of finish. They are mostly made in England or Germany, with other interesting fabrics coming from other countries such as South Africa. Take your time choosing the color: light or dark, traditional or contemporary. Do not look only at the pile and color, but examine the backing. Hold it up to the light; the good quality mohair should be closely woven and not too soft.

PAD FABRICS Think of which pad fabric you will use: natural materials or man-made ones. Look at upholstery fabrics used for miniature bears: sometimes you will find among them the right one to complement an unusually colored fur fabric. Consider the type of bear you are making—small or large, traditional or unusual—when you are choosing the fabrics, the embroidery thread for the nose, the eyes, the type of joints, and the stuffing.

PAD FABRICS

1 Suede, a natural material, for better looking bears.

2 Ultrasuede, a hard-wearing man-made fabric, available in a wide variety of colors.

3 Wool felt, a traditional pad material.

4 Suedette, an easy material to work with for beginners as it is less slippery.

5 Velvet, less commonly used, as it is difficult to sew and it frays.

FABRICS FOR MINIATURE BEARS

1 Short-hair upholstery fabric, available in many different colors; it is very easy to work with.

2 Cashmere. Very smooth, makes soft strokeable bears.

3 Long-hair upholstery fabric. Makes more furry miniature bears.

4 Very short sparse mohair, for miniature bears that look more like their bigger counterparts. Mohair is a bit more difficult to work with than upholstery fabric.

FUR FABRICS FOR BEARMAKING

1 Dense, extremely short mohair for small bears.

2 Sparse, short mohair for small bears—gives a "dishevelled" look.

3 Sparse, medium-length mohair, antique-style, for a wide range of bears.

4 Dense, medium-short mohair, used for traditional medium bears.

5 Sparse, feathery mohair, of the type often used in old bears, but which also looks good in modern-style bears.

6 Dense, long, "distressed" mohair, for larger bears with thick coats.

7 Extra-long wavy mohair for large bears.

8 Alpaca, a dense, rich wool, for quality bears.

9 Bouclé-style mohair for unusual bears.

10 Blue-dyed, sparse, feathery mohair for bears that are different.

11 Viscose, for contemporary, different bears.

12 Cotton fur fabric, used for cuddly bears.

13 Acrylic fur fabric, for children's bears.

STUFFINGS

1 Polyester filling, flat and heavy. It is clean and safe and produces well stuffed, heavy bears. Most popular stuffing, used for modern and for traditional bears.

2 Bouncy polyester filling. Also clean and safe, produces cuddly, lighter bears. Especially suited for bears for children.

3 Wood wool, which also used to be called "excelsior." Used for traditional, antique-style bears, and also for stuffing noses to make it easier to drive the needle through when embroidering the nose and putting glass eyes in.

4 Kapok, a natural material, widely used in antique bears, but less common now as its light, feathery fibers fly around and can be allergenic.

5 Plastic pellets. Very popular nowadays, it is more commonly placed only in the bear's body, to give it a slumped look. Often used in conjunction with other soft fillings. Not safe for children unless the pellets are first placed in a separate fabric bag which is securely closed.

6 Steel shot: very heavy, sometimes used in miniature bears. Do not use lead shot, which is poisonous.

7 Inserts for flexible limbs, made of plastic-coated wire inside a foam cover. They are placed inside arms and legs, attached to the joints, and padded with polyester stuffing. Not suitable for children's bears.

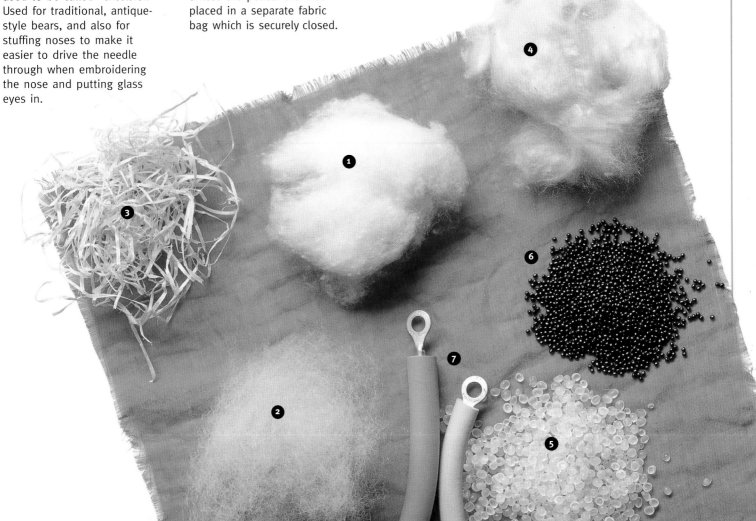

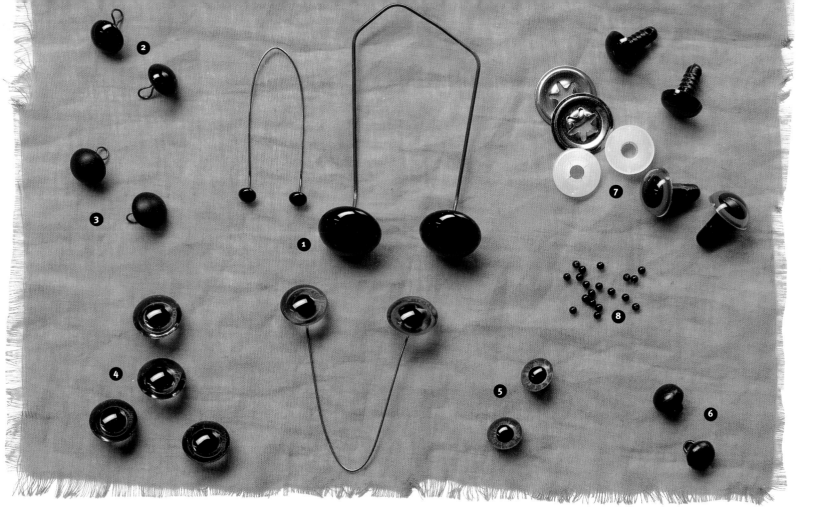

EYES

1 *Glass eyes on wires* come in many sizes and colors. The most economical of the glass eyes, they need to be separated and the wire twisted with pliers to make the loops.

Glass eyes with pre-formed loops are easier to use as the loop is already formed. There are several different types:

2 Black glass eyes, with a shiny finish are the most popular type. The ones here have a single-wire loop.

3 Sanded black eyes, with a dull finish, made to resemble the antique shoe button eyes.

4 Colored glass eyes, with double loops, come in a wide range of colors.

5 "Buzzard" eyes, with a handpainted, enameled animal-look pattern to the iris. More expensive but more realistic.

6 *Shoe button eyes*, a modern replica of the original antique ones.

7 *Plastic safety eyes*, for children's bears. They come in black or in colors, and they are closed with either metal or plastic washers.

8 *Onyx bead eyes* for miniature bears; semi-precious, perfectly round stone eyes.

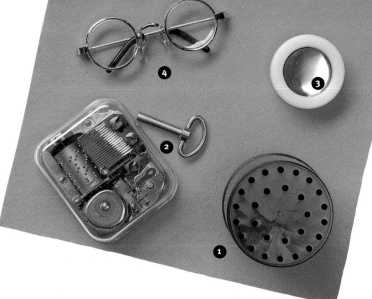

NOSES

Plastic safety noses, occasionally used for children's bears, but not really necessary because embroidered noses are safe as long as they are well secured.

◀ JOINTS

❶ Nut and bolt joints, available in many different sizes. Very strong, they can be used for all size bears, from small to extra-extra large.

❷ Cotter pin joints, also available in many different sizes, from ¼in upward.

❸ Plastic safety joints, also available in different sizes, and usable for any bears, not only children's.

❹ Double cotter pin joint. This is made up from two normal cotter pin joints, with two pins joined at the loop ends. They are used to achieve heads that move and droop, as in a worn bear.

❺ Swivel neck joint. Modern addition to the range of joints available that allows bears to move their heads into different, appealing positions.

▲ MISCELLANEOUS ITEMS

❶ Growler, available in different sizes.

❷ Musical movement, available in different traditional tunes, with wind-up key.

❸ Musical pushbutton, for placing in an ear or a paw, anywhere it can be activated with pressure.

❹ Spectacles, available in different styles.

Stitches

To start making a bear, all you need to know is the very basics of sewing. Here we describe the basic stitches needed for bearmaking, which are in fact very few. Ladder stitch, the most important stitch to learn, is described step by step on page 59.

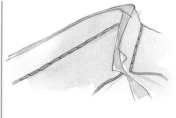

MACHINE STITCHING
For stitching the bear, a straight stitch is used, not too long or too short, using a medium tension.

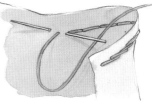

BACKSTITCH
If you choose to hand-stitch the bear, use small stitches close together.

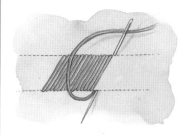

SATIN STITCH
Long flat stitches placed very close to each other; used for embroidering the nose.

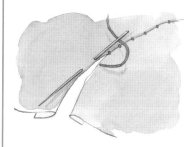

LADDER STITCH
An essential stitch, used to close openings, sew on ears, and generally used when a hidden stitch is required.

The question most often asked is whether the main seams of the bear should be sewn by hand or machine. The answer is either. There are advantages in using a machine: it is quicker and the stitches may be tighter and more even. However, on smaller bears hand stitching may be preferable, especially around tricky areas such as the head gusset and the footpads. If you choose to sew by hand then a small backstitch should be used, as the stitching must be continuous so that the seam is very firm when pushing fillings into the bear.

SEWING CLOTHES When making clothes for bears, the same applies: you can sew by hand if you prefer, but machine stitching is an easy way to achieve even, tight stitches which are quite secure.

Bear making techniques

The all important underlying foundations to build the better bear, from designing to stitching via pattern making.

Teddy Bear Design

Most Teddy Bear makers start by making bears from existing patterns. But sooner or later you will want to design your own bears. A good starting point is to study the shapes and proportions of existing Teddy Bears, new and old. In addition, it is extremely helpful to observe real bears, either by visiting a zoo, or by studying photographs in books or magazines.

Designing a Teddy Bear is not a difficult task. Knowing how to draw is not the most important thing; the first requirement is to be "able to see," to visualize the final product that you want to achieve. It is important to get a "feel" for the bear's outline, shape, and proportion, and perceive the differences between the real thing and a toy. Once this is accomplished, drawing the actual patterns will be easy.

However, the new designer should not assume that the first bear made will come out exactly as expected. Techniques will have to be learned, and shapes refined. Even experienced professional designers will work through several versions of a design before they are satisfied with the final product.

Designing a Teddy Bear comes somewhere between designing a doll and designing a stuffed animal. It is drawn from the perspective of the profile in silhouette, as most stuffed animals are, although because it is drawn standing upright, with jointed arms and legs, its shape is much more like that of a doll.

It is important to understand that patterns are a flat representation, while a stuffed bear is a three-dimensional object. Paper patterns have to incorporate an extra dimension to allow for the roundness of the shape. Initially this means adding an extra half-inch or so all around the patterns. Gussets are an important device used to add extra bulk, as on the head. Other specific shaping can be achieved through darts.

OBSERVING BEARS AND TRACING THEIR SHAPE

The first task is to become familiar with the shapes of real bears and see how they relate to those of stuffed bears. To achieve this, start by tracing different bear shapes, as a useful exercise in "learning to see."

1 Carefully observe the proportions of a real bear: its massive body, thick neck, long muzzle, small eyes and ears, powerful haunches, long arms and legs. Notice how a bear sits and stands, how its shape changes as it moves, how its ears are mobile and face different directions as its attention shifts. Note the flat head and how the position of the head in relation to the body differs from that of a human being. Some bears have a noticeable hump on the back, just below the neck.

2 | Choose a photograph of a real bear and trace around it to get a feeling for its shape. Repeat this with several bear photographs.

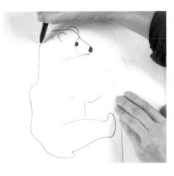

3 | If your photographs are small, enlarge them with a photocopier. A black and white reproduction will do, as you are interested mostly in the outline and not the fine detail. Trace around the enlargements.

4 | If the bear is standing on four legs, turn it sideways so it looks as if it is sitting. Most likely the head will not be in the right position. Cut out the paper tracing and turn the head so it faces forward. Join up the broken lines to complete a curved neck.

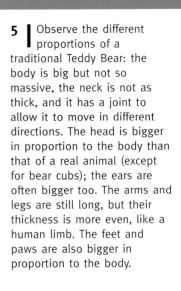

5 | Observe the different proportions of a traditional Teddy Bear: the body is big but not so massive, the neck is not as thick, and it has a joint to allow it to move in different directions. The head is bigger in proportion to the body than that of a real animal (except for bear cubs); the ears are often bigger too. The arms and legs are still long, but their thickness is more even, like a human limb. The feet and paws are also bigger in proportion to the body.

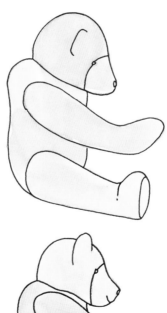

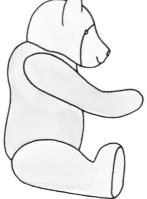

6 | Trace these Teddies as well, and notice the difference between them and real bears.

THE BODY AND LIMBS

For our example of basic pattern-making, we will take a Teddy Bear of "average" proportions, in which the body is about half the total height, the head is about half the size of the body, and the arms and legs are either the same length or a little shorter than the body. After mastering the design of an "average" bear, you can experiment by varying the proportions.

YOU WILL NEED

For the pattern design
Paper
Pencil
Ruler

---

1 We will start by designing the body, as its dimensions are the easiest to calculate: about half the desired total height of the bear. Using this figure, we will design the arms and legs, and finally, the head. As they are jointed to the body by overlapping them, the arms will look longer than the body, and the legs will look shorter. To obtain the final working pattern, you will need to add about one inch to each pattern piece measurement, to allow for the roundness of the bear and the seam allowances. It is best to add this now, before constructing the patterns.

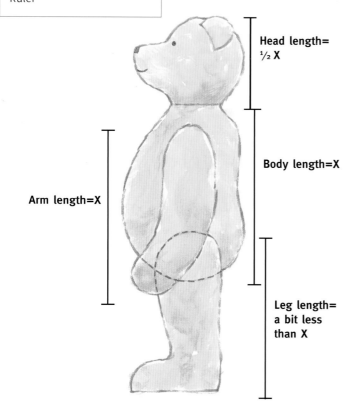

Head length= ½ X

Arm length=X

Body length=X

Leg length= a bit less than X

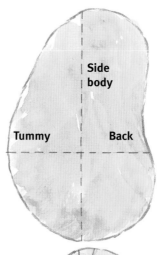

Side body

Tummy   Back

Dart

Side body

Tummy   Back

Dart

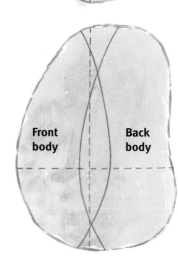

Front body   Back body

2 The *body* pattern is designed from a side profile view. The tummy and bottom are emphasized; the chest area is made a little flatter; a hump can be added for a more realistic shape. The width of the body is about two-thirds of its height. The seams will be in the center of the back and the front.

3 Extra shaping can be added by darts to emphasize the shoulders and enlarge the tummy area. To achieve this effect, cut the original body shape in half, pull the pieces apart, and draw the darts.

4 The body can also be made in four parts rather than just two, with extra seams on the sides. This is also made by cutting the original body in half, pulling the pieces apart, and drawing matching curved sides instead of the straight line. The front and back side lines are usually the same.

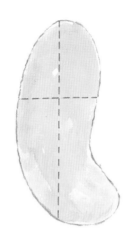

5 The *arms* are about the same length as the body —about one-third of its width, and the paw should be slightly curved.

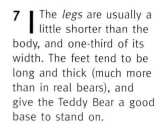

7 The *legs* are usually a little shorter than the body, and one-third of its width. The feet tend to be long and thick (much more than in real bears), and give the Teddy Bear a good base to stand on.

8 Legs also come in a variety of alternative shapes. The joined leg which is then folded in half is very common.

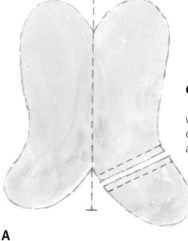

A

6 (A&B) Alternative arm shapes are often used, where the outer and inner part of the arms are joined, either along the back seams or the front seams. The inner part of the arm has a separate paw made from a non-furry material. Make the paw pattern by cutting off the lower part of one side of the arm (which will be its inner side), and then adding seam allowances to the two pieces so that when joined together later they will still form one complete arm.

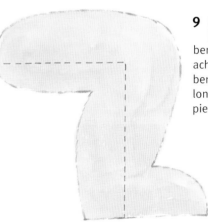

9 Modern Teddy Bears are sometimes made with bent legs. This can be achieved by either designing a bent leg, or by using an extra long leg and placing a flexible piece of armature inside it.

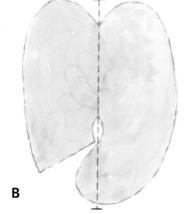

B

3/4 of foot length

10 For the footpad, trace a line about $3/4$ of the length of the foot. Trace another at right angles, about $2/3$ of the length of the first. Complete the footpad by drawing an oval shape around the two lines.

THE HEAD AND ITS GUSSET

The *head* is the most important part of the bear so it is worth paying a lot of attention to its design. The profile head forms only the side of the head; a *head gusset* has to be designed to fit between the two side heads and give it both its size and the characteristic shape of the Teddy Bear head.

YOU WILL NEED
To design the head pattern
Paper
Pen or pencil
Piece of string
Scissors

1 | The basic dimensions of the side heads are: (A) the top to neck measurement, which is approximately half that of the body, or one quarter of the total height of the bear, and (B), the nose to back measurement, which is around one and a quarter times (A). Each *gusset* is drawn to match a particular head. It runs from the tip of the nose to the back neck edge of the head. It has a relatively straight and narrow shape in the nose area. At the eye point, it widens rapidly to its maximum width at the top of the head. Then it tapers gently to a narrower width at the back of the neck. The maximum width of the gusset is around two-thirds of measurement (A) of the head.

2 | To design a gusset for a particular head, first use a piece of string to carefully measure the distance (C) between the tip of the nose and the back of the head, along the top side of the head.

4 | Place the folded strip on a table, fold downward. Decide the width of the nose area, and mark half this measurement along one short edge of the strip, starting from the folded edge. Place the side head on the strip, matching the nose point to the paper fold. Transfer the gusset width mark onto the head.

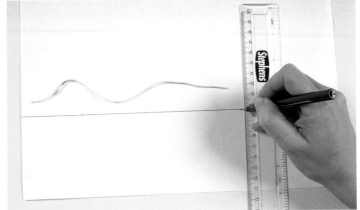

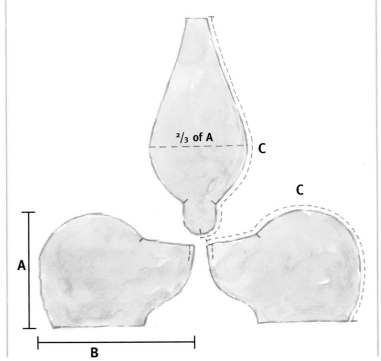

²/₃ of A

C

C

A

B

3 | On a piece of paper, mark and cut a rectangle, with the length the (C) measurement above, and the width, that of the desired gusset, which is usually two-thirds of the (A) measurement of the head. Then fold the paper in half lengthwise. The fold represents the very center of the head.

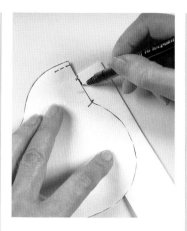

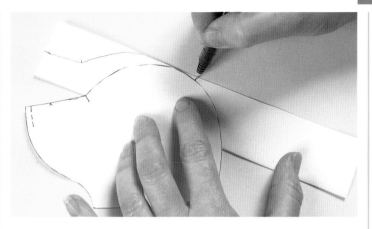

5 Mark a point ⅛in to ¼in below the nose width point, and match the gusset width point on the head to the second point. Hold the head in place, and trace a line on the folded paper, just up to the "eye" point (where the side head profile starts curving).

7 Continue sliding the head along the strip, tracing the gusset as you go along. After leaving the edge of the paper, just make dots as you slide and turn the head. The last dot should be short of the end of the paper, and a little way up from the folded edge.

11 Then check the gusset from the "eye" point to the neck at the back. The length may need a slight adjustment, but do allow a certain amount of ease onto the gusset, to make a more rounded head.

9 Continue by rounding off the corner of the nose end of the gusset.

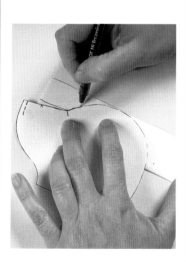

6 Shift the head just a fraction, so that the highest point on the head touches the edge of the paper. Trace that curve.

8 Join the points with a gently rounded line. It should have a tapered shape. From the last point, draw a short straight line toward the folded edge, to complete the width of the gusset.

10 Cut the gusset out, open it up, and check it against the head, nose end first. Match the center point of the nose (on the gusset fold) to the *seam allowance* point on the head. The "eye" points should match.

12 The ears are basically a "D" shape. They can be drawn bigger or smaller, or more, or less, rounded. There is no "right size" for ears, it very much depends on the particular bear expression you want to create.

Patterns

Patterns form the basis for making a Teddy Bear and

you will need to understand how they work, whether

you use one of the many commercially

available ones, or whether you

design your own. They are drawn

on paper, and have distinct

marks which provide

instructions for their use.

Patterns represent each and every part of the bear: side head and head gusset, ears, body, arms and paws, legs and footpads. Original pattern pieces should never be cut. They should be traced or photocopied and then kept on file for future reference.

PATTERN SIZE Usually, commercial patterns are printed in their full size. However, sometimes when the patterns appear in a book, they have to be reduced in size, so that they can fit on the page. If they have been reduced, they will have to be enlarged again to their original size before making the bear, either by using a photocopier or a grid technique (see right).

Once the patterns are available on paper in full size, it is recommended that they are glued to cardboard to reinforce them and make them less likely to wear when used frequently. If the patterns are traced rather than photocopied, you should make sure that any marks and instructions on the original are transferred to the copy.

☞
**Positioning eyes,
pages 66–71
Marking positions of
joints, pages 52–3**

REPRODUCING AND
UNDERSTANDING
PATTERNS
Not all the stages explained here will need to be used for every pattern. Choose the ones that are relevant to the set of patterns you are using at the time. Whatever method you use, the aim is to obtain a set of patterns that will include every part of the bear to be cut from the fabric.

1 The easiest way of enlarging a pattern is to use a photocopier. The pieces would have originally been reduced by a certain proportion, and the instructions should provide information on how much to enlarge them by to make them the original size. This is expressed either by a percentage ("enlarge to 200%") or by page size ("enlarge from 8in x 10in to 9in x 12in").

2 In the grid method, a grid of lines about $\frac{1}{2}$in apart is drawn over the copied patterns. A larger grid of lines $\frac{3}{4}$in or 1in apart is drawn on another sheet of paper. The points where the patterns cross the grid lines are marked and reproduced on the larger grid. The points are then joined with pencil lines, reproducing the original pattern.

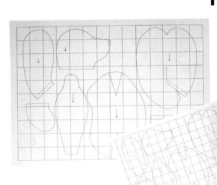

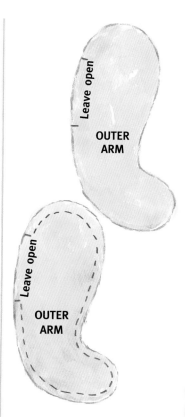

OUTER ARM

OUTER ARM

3 Each piece is usually labeled with the name of the part. The solid line on the outside edge of the pattern is the cutting line, and should always be traced. Cut the paper pattern pieces on this outside line. The stitching line is usually ¼in in from the edge, and it is marked with a dotted line. However, Teddy Bear patterns do not always have the stitching lines marked; in those that don't, a ¼in seam allowance is assumed. The more important marks are those that indicate where there should be *no* stitching, to leave openings for turning and stuffing the bear. Make sure to transfer those to your working pattern.

4 In commercial patterns, dots and crosses are used to indicate the points where the eyes and the joints should go. They can be used as a guide, but are not always completely accurate because they depend on the way the stitching is carried out by the particular maker; a small amount of deviation can be expected. Placement also depends on the size of the joints chosen, and on where the eyes look best when the bear is made. When you design your own pattern, you have to find those positions by yourself, so the way to determine the eye and joint placement points is explained in the relevant sections.

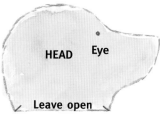

HEAD Eye

Leave open

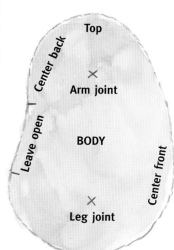

Top

Center back

Arm joint

Leave open

BODY

Center front

Leave open

Leg joint

5 The other important mark is the arrow that indicates the direction of the pile of the fur fabric. This direction is based on the way animal fur goes—down or sideways on the body, down on the legs and arms, outward from the nose on the head, and up on the ears. The arrows on the pattern pieces indicate the way they should be placed on the fabric; they should point in the same direction as the pile of the fur.

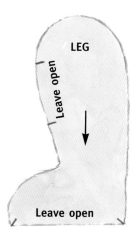

LEG

Leave open

Leave open

Leave open

EAR

6 When sewing ordinary fabric, two layers are often cut at the same time. This is not possible with fur fabric, where each piece has to be cut separately. Therefore it is very important to be aware that to obtain pieces that will match when placed right sides together for stitching, some of the pieces have to be reversed. This is also important to achieve left and right sides in the bear's limbs. Most patterns actually indicate how many pieces have to be cut, and if any need reversing.

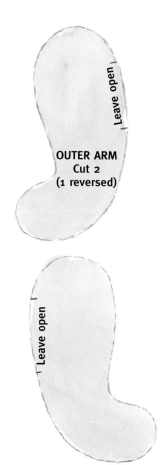

Leave open

OUTER ARM Cut 2 (1 reversed)

Leave open

Fabric Layout, Marking, and Cutting

Equipped with a set of patterns to make a bear, we have to choose the fabrics, and lay out the patterns on the back, with the pieces reversed as required. The patterns are then traced around with a marker that shows clearly, and cut out.

For collectors' bears, mohair is usually used, a pure wool fabric with a pile, or nap. The pile can be short, long, dense, sparse, straight, wavy, or "distressed" (roughed up so fibers go in different directions).

First establish the direction of the pile of the fur fabric. In "distressed" mohairs the direction is determined by looking at the edges of the fabric and checking from which edge the pile comes away from, and which edge it overhangs.

PLACEMENT The pattern pieces are placed on the back side of the fur fabric, reversed when required. An easy way to remember the numbers of, and the reversing of the pieces, is to draw as many copies of the pattern pieces as are necessary, and draw in reverse the ones that require it: for example, two side heads (one reversed), etc. As mohair fabric is rather expensive, it is best to place all the pieces before you cut anything, interlocking them like a jigsaw puzzle, to make the most economical use of the fabric, and to make sure that you have enough fabric. However, make sure that you do not get carried away and

☞
**Bear fabrics, pages 14–18
Tools and equipment,
pages 10–13**

while attempting to save fabric, you turn the pieces upside down instead of sideways by mistake, and end up with the fur pile going in the wrong direction.

The bear's paws and pads are often made out of a different material such as felt, suede, the reverse of the mohair, or with the fibers plucked out. Although these materials do not have a nap as clearly as the fur fabric does, pieces cut in different directions could look as if they had different shades of the same color. Therefore it is best to cut all the pieces in the *same* direction, although the *actual* direction is less important.

The patterns are then traced onto the fabric with a suitable marker, and any relevant marks are also transferred.

CUTTING The fabric is usually cut with small sharp pointed scissors. Mohair pile fabric must be cut with great care, snipping the back only, not the pile, or you will end up with a bear with "bare" patches along the seams. After cutting, the pile will pull apart easily when the piece is removed. Other cutting instruments can be used, such as scalpels or sharp craft knives. Rotary cutters are unsuitable as the pressure cannot be accurately controlled and they will most likely cut the pile as well as the back.

FABRIC LAYOUT AND MARKING

Before cutting the pattern pieces to make the bear, the direction of the pile, or nap of the fabric, should be established, the patterns laid out with the correct pieces reversed, and the pieces clearly drawn on the reverse side of the fabric.

1 To find the nap, stroke the fabric with your hand in different directions. The pile should feel smooth and soft when stroked in the right direction; when stroked in any other direction, the fibers are pulled upward and will feel rough. Draw an arrow indicating the direction of the pile on the back of the fabric as a reminder.

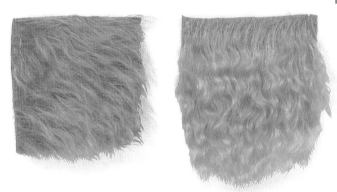
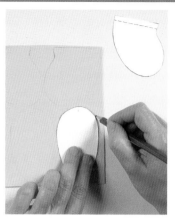

2 | In mohair fur fabric, the pile usually goes in the direction of the straight weave of the fabric backing, and parallel to the selvage, but sometimes it can go diagonally. With "distressed" mohair, look at the edges and see whether the pile comes away from it or overhangs it.

3 | Carefully place all the pieces, except paws and pads, on the back of the fur fabric, reversing where required. Check that all the pieces are there and that all reversing is done sideways, "mirror image," so that the direction of the pile is correct.

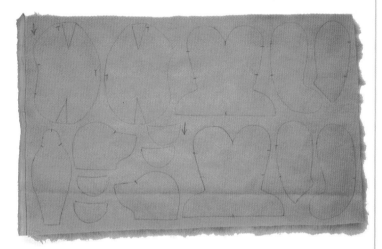

4 | Mark the pieces onto the back of the fabric with a soft pencil or a ballpoint pen. Transfer the most important marks, such as the openings and any others that will help make sense of the bear pieces once they are cut: for example, a "T" for Top and for Tummy in the body will make it easy to tell which way the body goes. Copy eye and joint positions if your pattern has them, but treat them as general indicators only, not as definitive placements.

5 | The paws and the footpads are traced and cut onto a piece of Ultrasuede, felt, or suede. These materials sometimes have no right or wrong side, and you can choose which side to use. Always place the pattern pieces so that the fabric is going in the same direction.

6 | If you are using dark colored fabric, where a pen or a pencil marking will not show, try using a white correcting pen. This also helps to prevent fabric fraying.

CUTTING FUR FABRIC

When cutting fur fabric, the important thing is to cut the backing and not the pile of the fabric. Therefore it is best cut with small sharp pointed scissors, and not with big dressmaking scissors.

YOU WILL NEED

For cutting fur fabric

Mohair fur fabric, with pattern pieces marked on the back

Small sharp pointed scissors

Alternative: scalpel or craft knife

1 | Hold the fabric and slide the point of the small sharp scissors under the back of the fur fabric, well clear of the pile. Snip the back with short strokes. You may go slowly at the beginning, but with practice you will soon gain speed. When the piece is cut, pull it away and the pile fibers will separate easily.

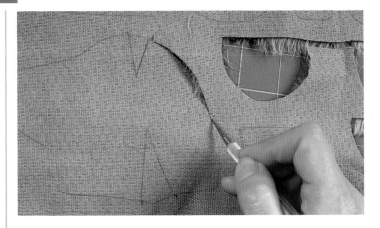

2 | An alternative to cutting with scissors is to use a scalpel. You will need to learn to control its pressure to avoid cutting the pile, but once learned, it can lead to clean, accurate cutting. Use a self-healing cutting mat underneath. Scalpels can be useful when cutting several bears in one sitting, to rest the hand by changing its position. Be very careful with scalpels though, as they are very sharp, and make sure they are never left within reach of children.

3 | When all the pieces are cut, arrange them on a table in "bear" position, to check that all the pieces required are there, and that they are correctly reversed.

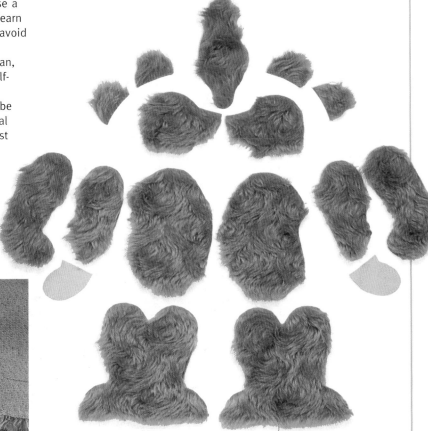

Stitching the Bear

Once all the parts are correctly cut, it is time to put the bear together by stitching the pieces. Right and left pieces are matched, pinned, and stitched together to make the different parts of the bear: body, head and ears, arms, and legs. The bear is taking shape and becoming a little more real.

Stitching the bear can be done either by hand or by machine. If you are stitching by hand, use a strong thread, a needle with a fairly large eye, and a small back stitch. If you stitch by machine, use normal thread and a medium-size stitch. Here we will assume that the bear is stitched by machine. Be sure to match all parts correctly, and to stitch evenly, keeping the fabrics flat.

THREAD The color of the thread should roughly match the color of the fur fabric, but the match does not have to be absolutely exact, as the fur fabric is likely to hide the thread.

PINNING THE PIECES Most people prefer to pin the pieces together before stitching. It is recommended that colored-headed pins are used, so that they cannot get lost in the fur. Place the pins at a right angle to the fabric, so they are easy to remove as you stitch. Some people do not pin at all, or use just a minimum to hold crucial spots together. Still others prefer to tack the pieces in place before stitching. Use whatever method suits you best, or a combination—for example, pin the difficult pieces, and tack the fussy ones like the head gusset and the footpads.

Use the point of a needle, pin or seam-ripper to push the pile of the fabric inward as you go along, and bring the fabric edges together. This will make it easier to tease the hairs out at the seams from the right side, after the bear is stitched.

PINNING AND STITCHING THE BODY

TWO-PIECE BODY

We start by putting together the bear's body. Shown here are techniques for making two types of bodies: a two-piece body with darts, and a four-piece body.

1 If the body has darts, first fold the darts, fur sides together so that the marked lines match. Pin the resulting triangular shape with colored-headed pins placed along the marked line. If your two-piece body pattern does not have darts, ignore steps 1–2 and go straight to 3–4.

2 Machine stitch the darts first, carefully removing the pins as you work. Make sure you reverse or knot the thread before cutting the ends off, so that the stitching does not become undone.

3 Cut off the excess fabric of the dart, leaving a seam allowance of between $\frac{1}{8}$in and $\frac{1}{4}$in (depending on the bear size). Place the two body pieces together, making sure that the tummies and the back openings match. Pin the body if you wish, but leave the back opening unpinned.

4 Start machine stitching at one of the opening points. Stitch around the bear body, leaving a $\frac{1}{4}$in seam allowance, removing the pins as you go along. Stop at the other end of the back opening.

FOUR-PIECE BODY

A four-piece body gives a more rounded bear body. First the two front pieces are joined together along the center front seam, then the back pieces are joined along the center back seam (leaving an opening for turning), and finally the front is joined to the back at the side seams, pinned and stitched all around.

YOU WILL NEED
Four-piece body
Bear body pieces, cut in fur fabric
Matching color thread
Sewing machine, with a size 14 (90) needle
Colored-headed pins
Small sharp scissors

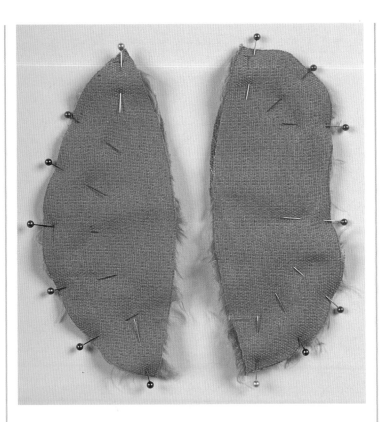

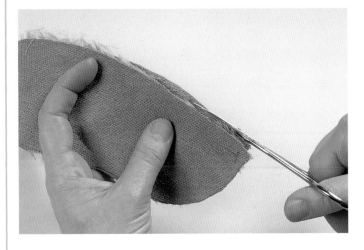

1 | Place the two back pieces, fur sides together and match them carefully. Accuracy of cutting is more important in a four-piece body, so make sure that the size of the two pieces is exactly the same. If not, carefully trim off any excess fabric so they match perfectly. Repeat with the two front pieces.

2 | Start pinning each pair of matching pieces together at one corner, and push the fur inward as you pin.

3 | Pin together the front piece along the center front seam tummy only, from the top corner (neck) to the lower corner (bottom). Pin together the back piece along the center back, leaving an opening for turning.

4 | Machine stitch the two front pieces together, starting at one corner, removing the pins as you go along.

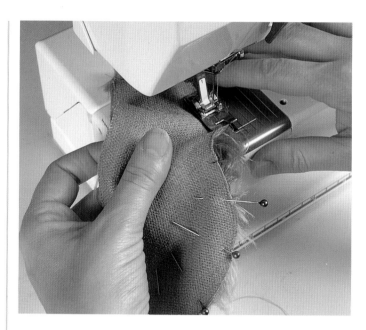

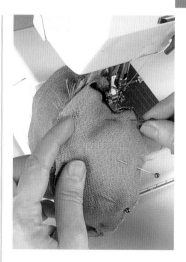

7 Stitch all around this seam, taking care to open the seam allowances at the top and bottom ends. Sew slowly at those points as you will be stitching four layers of fur fabric at the same time.

5 Machine stitch the two back pieces together, starting at one corner, leaving the back opening unstitched.

6 Open up the front and back pieces, place them fur sides together, matching the seams at the top and bottom, and pinning them. Leave a small gap at the top for the neck joint, but no others, as the stuffing opening is already on the back seam.

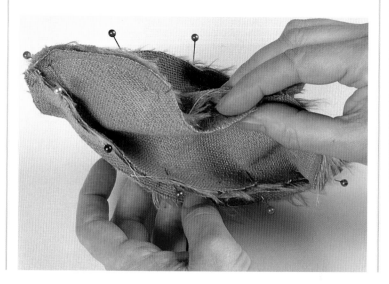

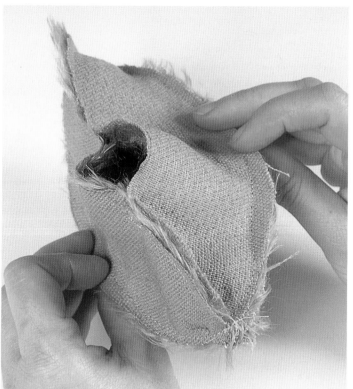

8 The body is now complete. You can clearly see the back opening through which it will be turned.

Stitching the Head

The head is the most important part of the bear. It is what we look at first—not only the features (eyes, nose, ears), but also the shape of the head. The first step in achieving a nicely shaped head is to stitch the side heads and the gusset well and evenly.

Before you start to sew the seams, consider what sort of finish you want to achieve. If you are using a long pile mohair, you may want to trim some of the pile away before starting. Be careful where you cut, and remove fibers from the area of the seam allowance only. You must be very accurate sewing the seams.

Always stitch the pieces with their right sides together. Sew with a straight stitch and remember to leave an even seam allowance of about ¼in. The precise size is not so important, but once you have decided on a width for the seam allowance, stick to that throughout, or the pieces will be uneven. If you don't have a sewing machine then hand sew with small back stitches using a good straight needle. Always use good quality sewing thread: ordinary polyester/cotton thread is fine for the main seams; there is no need to use extra strong thread.

Some fabrics that are very slippery, or ones that "travel" can be held together with a few colored-headed pins while you are sewing. Never use ordinary pins as these may get lost in the fabric. If the pile is very long, it may be better not to tack or put pins in, but easier to tuck the pile in as you sew instead. Do not try to sew too much at one time, but keep control of your machine and sew slowly and steadily.

With fabrics that fray, oversew the edges first, or use a little fray check liquid or white craft glue to seal the edges before stitching.

When you start stitching by machine, hold the pieces in place by inserting the needle first; once the needle is in place then the two pieces of fabric cannot move. Get into the habit of always putting the needle in before lowering the presser foot.

THE HEAD GUSSET
Inserting the head gusset is the most important part of sewing your bear. The seams are right in the middle of the head and, as a result, right in the center of the face, the focal point of the bear. If they are off center then the bear's face will look crooked and affect its whole character.

YOU WILL NEED
Inserting the head gusset
Pattern pieces cut in your chosen fabric
Sewing machine or needle for hand stitching
Matching color thread
Colored-headed pins
Sharp pointed scissors

☞
Introduction to Stitching the Bear—The Body, pages 33–35

---

1 The parts of the head are two side heads, one cut reversed, and one head gusset, which fits between the two side heads.

2 Place the two side head pieces right sides together. Use pins to hold the material if you wish, but it is easier to push the pile in if you do not. Place these pieces in the machine, lower the needle to hold them together, and then clamp with the presser foot. Secure with a few stitches in reverse first.

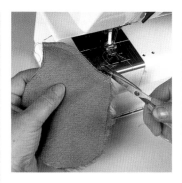

3 Start sewing at the nose, working toward the neck edge. Finish the seam with another few back stitches and then cut the thread.

5 Put the machine needle in through the gusset and center seam to hold them in place. Lower the presser foot and sew around the end of the gusset. Always start at the nose and work toward the neck edge, and sew one half first and then the other.

7 Restart about two inches along the seam making sure that the edges are in the right place, and that the two pieces finish at the neck edge evenly. Sew to the end, do a few back stitches, and then cut the thread.

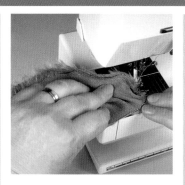

8 Start at the nose again to do the other side. If your bear has a very square muzzle, this is where the shaping is done. As you sew across the end make a point, turning the fabric at a 90° angle to make a nice sharp corner.

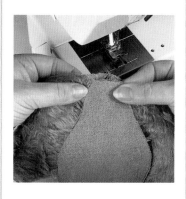

4 Find the center of the nose end of the head gusset piece; mark the spot if you wish. Place this center mark exactly on the seam that you have just sewn in the side head pieces. Remember to put right sides together.

6 If you are using nut and bolt joints or safety joints, you will need to leave an opening in the seam; do this about midway along the top of the head, just behind where the ears are likely to be placed. Take a few back stitches to secure and then cut the thread.

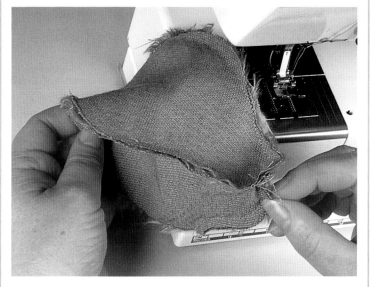

9 Sew straight to the end, as you need to leave an opening on one seam only. The head gusset should now be in place.

HEAD DARTS

These are sometimes used to give shape and definition to the bear's head. There are two ways of stitching darts: the first one is to fold the fabric, matching the dart lines, and stitch along the lines. Then the surplus fabric is cut. This method is demonstrated in the section showing how to stitch a two-piece body with darts. Another way is to cut out the triangular dart shape first, and then stitch it. This second method is described here.

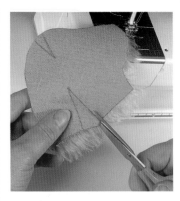

1 Using very sharp scissors cut out the dart shaped pieces. Only cut the backing and not the pile.

☞

Stitching a two-piece body with darts, page 33

YOU WILL NEED
To stitch darts
Pattern pieces cut in your chosen fabric, with darts in the side heads
Sewing machine or needle for hand stitching
Matching color thread
Colored-headed pins
Sharp pointed scissors

2 Remove the pieces; the pile will just peel away.

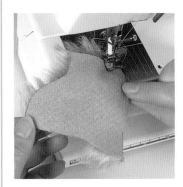

3 Fold, right sides together matching the dart edges, and sew along the side leaving a ¼in seam allowance Start sewing from the edge toward the point.

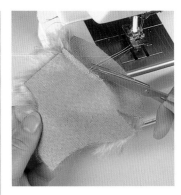

4 Do a few back stitches and cut the thread. Now finish the second dart in the same way.

5 The finished darts show the added shape. Repeat the procedure for the other side head, and then follow the same steps explained in the previous section to join the two side heads together and insert the gusset.

STITCHING THE EARS

The ears are stitched along the curved edge only, leaving the straight side open for turning. Because the fur fabric fiber goes upward in the ears, it is necessary to take extra care in pushing the pile inward as you stitch. If you are using pins, place them at right angles to the edge of the fabric. Some ears have a dart in their inner side, to help the ear curve more after stitching.

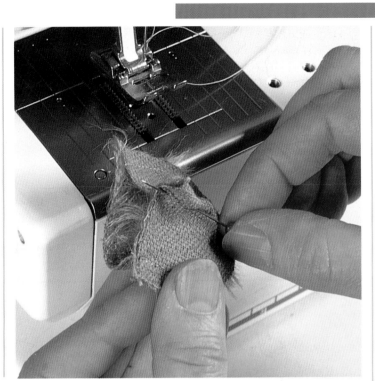

YOU WILL NEED

To stitch the ears
Pair of ear pieces
Sewing machine or needle for hand stitching
Matching color thread
Colored-headed pins
Seam ripper or thick needle

1 | Place two ear pieces fur sides together, and pin the curved sides at right angles to the edge of the fabric. If your ear has a dart in its inner side, match one straight piece with one darted piece, but do not stitch the dart yet.

2 | Stitch the curved edge by machine with a ¼in seam allowance, removing the pins as you go, and pushing the hair in quite thoroughly with the point of a seam ripper or a thick needle. Repeat for the second ear.

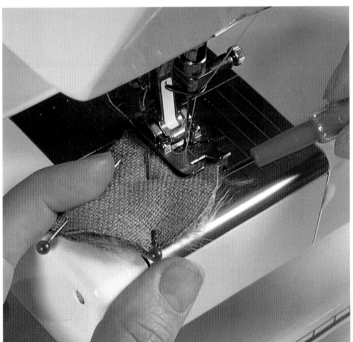

3 | If the ear has a dart on its inner side, pin and stitch this dart after the curved seam is stitched, then cut off the excess fabric. You can also use the other method of cutting the dart out first, and stitching the seam afterward, but take into account that the effect will be slightly different, with the inner ear becoming smaller and producing a tighter curve.

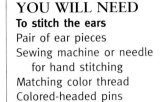

☞
Stitching darts in a two-piece body, page 33
Stitching darts in side head, page 38

SEWING THE ARMS

The pattern pieces for the arms can be cut in several different ways, but the principle of sewing them is the same. A common fault when sewing the arm is to pull one side more than the other when sewing around the curves. This can lead to the arm being twisted, turning the paw outward. Make sure the pieces are in the correct place before sewing and keep them under control.

☞

Types of arm shapes, in Designing the Bear section, pages 24–25

1 | Arm shapes can vary, but in all cases the first step is to stitch the paw pad to the inner arm. Arm stitching will be demonstrated here on a one-piece arm that has been cut with the seam running down the back, which is the type that poses most problems for bear makers.

YOU WILL NEED

For sewing the arms
Arm pieces cut in fur fabric
Paw pad piece cut in flat fabric—Ultrasuede, wool felt
Sewing machine or needle for hand stitching
Matching color thread
Colored-headed pins
Sharp pointed scissors

2 | With long pile fur, trim the seam allowance where the pad material is to be sewn on.

3 | Right sides together, place the pad on the end of the arm, matching the short straight edges, and checking that the two arm sides will match properly when the arm is folded in the next stage.

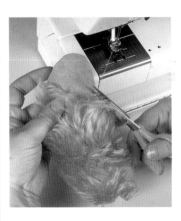

4 | Sew together and then do a few back stitches to secure. Cut the thread.

5 | Fold the arm in half with right sides together. With very long pile fabric, or to help prevent any twisting when sewing, place a few colored-headed pins along the arm at a right angle to the seam. Start to sew at the fold.

6 | Carefully sew around the end of the arm to attach the paws. Remove the pins as you come to them, and push the pile in.

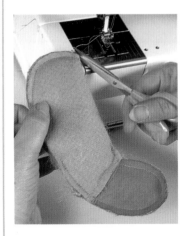

7 | Leave an opening on the back seam for putting the joints in and stuffing, and start to sew again about two inches further along around the shoulder area. Finish off, back at the other end of the fold.

SEWING SUEDE PADS

Suede is a natural material and it is very hard wearing. It can enhance the look and quality of your bear. Sewing suede by machine can be difficult if not approached in the right way. Using the method shown here makes it a lot easier.

YOU WILL NEED

For sewing suede pads

Arm pieces cut in fur fabric
Paw pad piece cut in
   suede
Sewing machine or needle
   for hand stitching
Matching colored thread
Piece of thin paper
Sharp pointed scissors

1 This pattern piece for the arm has a seam running down the front. The suede pad still has to be stitched on first.

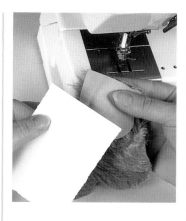

2 Trim the arm seam allowance as before and place right sides together, then place a piece of thin paper on top of the suede.

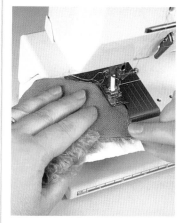

3 Turn over the fabric and paper and put the three layers under the presser foot and hold in place with the needle. Sew along the seam. Cut the thread and remove the paper. You will find that the paper will slide through and that the suede does not come into contact with the sewing machine at all and therefore will not stick.

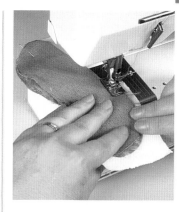

4 Sew the main seam as before using a piece of paper under the pad.

5 If using cotter pin joints, you can leave the opening at the top of the shoulder instead of on the back seam. Finish off.

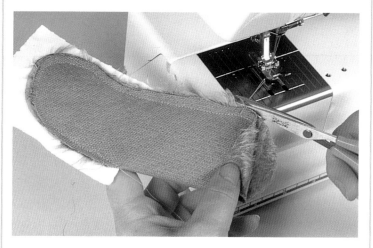

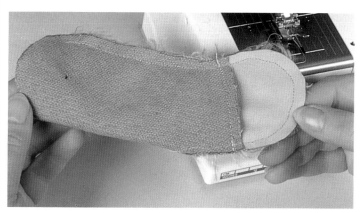

6 Peel the paper away, and the suede pad will be neatly stitched in place.

SEWING THE LEGS

As with the arms, the leg pattern pieces will take different forms, and be either in one or two pieces. Decide before stitching what type of joints you wish to use, and remember to leave the correct opening as you sew.

☞

Types of leg shapes, in Designing the Bear section, pages 24–25 Hidden limb opening for cotter pin joints, page 56

YOU WILL NEED

For sewing the legs
Leg pieces
Footpad piece cut in flat fabric—suede, Ultrasuede, wool felt
Sewing machine or needle for hand stitching
Matching color thread
Colored-headed pins
Piece of thin paper
Sharp pointed scissors

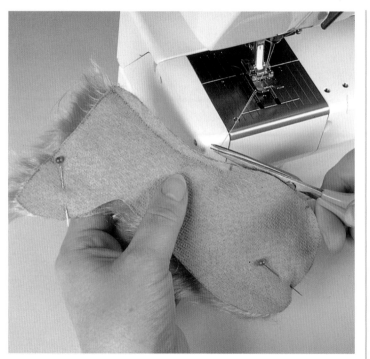

1 | To stitch a two-piece leg, place the pieces right sides together, and hold in place with a few colored-headed pins to prevent sliding. Start stitching on the back of the leg, at the lower edge.

2 | Leave an opening in the back seam for stuffing and inserting the joints. Sew halfway along the back seam and finish off.

3 | Start again about two inches further on and then sew around the top and down to the front of the foot. Do not sew across the end of the foot—leave it open to insert the footpads.

4 | Many legs come in one piece, with the two halves joined together. Fold the leg along the center back line, right sides together, and sew from the foot toward the top of the leg.

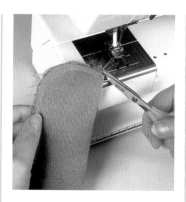

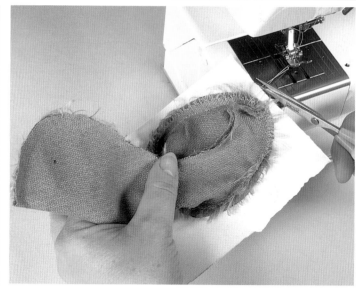

5 | Either leave the top of the leg open, or, as shown here, sew right around to the end. This will enable you to insert a cotter pin joint that will not be visible, as explained later in the section on joints. This method cannot be used if you use nut and bolt or safety joints. Finish off well and cut the thread.

7 | Start at the toe. Make sure that the middle of the footpad is exactly on the leg seam. Put the needle in first to secure the three layers, then lower the presser foot.

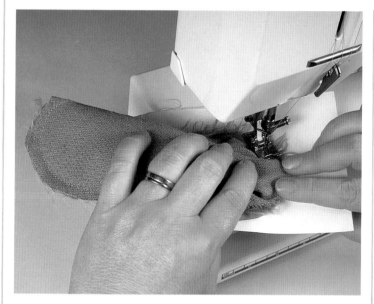

6 | Regardless of whether the leg is in one or two pieces, the footpad is inserted and stitched in the same way. Here we will show stitching a suede footpad using paper, as shown for the paw pads. Place the footpad onto a piece of thin paper and then stand the leg upright on top. Remember to place right sides together.

8 | Slowly guide the foot around, sewing a little at a time and leaving a ¼in seam allowance. If you use pins, they may get in the way. It is better to get used to holding your fabric and letting the machine do the work.

9 | Sew all the way around and overlap the first stitches to secure them. If you want your bear to stand, put in cardboard inserts, which should be the same size and shape as the footpad minus the seam allowance. In this case it is better to sew around the pad twice to reinforce it.

10 | Turn the leg over and peel the paper off the bottom, starting with the outer section and then the inner disk that remains.

Assembling the bear

The bear bones:
jointing and
stuffing for
mobility and
poseability,
shaping and
growling.

Putting Joints in the Bear

One of the Teddy Bear's most characteristic features is the use of rotating joints, which allows it to sit, move its arms and legs, and generally to be posed in all sorts of interesting ways. This feature makes it look more like a human being than an animal.

The joints are composed of pairs of disks, one of which goes inside the head, arm, or leg, and the other one inside the body. They are joined together, very tightly, through the fur fabric, by different means: cotter pin, bolts, or plastic stems, and secured in place by either twisting the pins' ends, screwing a nut on the bolt, or putting a one-way washer on the plastic stem.

There are other specialized joints and ways of jointing, such as the swivel neck joint which allows the head to be posed in many more interesting ways and the double split pin joint which is used to produce a slumped-head effect. The method of fixing swivel neck joints is explained later in this section. The thread joint is explained in the Miniature Bears section.

The three main types of joint, nut and bolt, cotter pin, and plastic safety joints are all very good. They all do an excellent job of keeping the bear's head and limbs in place, but are suitable for different purposes.

We will explain how the different joints fit together, and how they are closed and tightened, by first showing it done in small pieces of fabric.

☞

**Deciding on joint size and position, page 52
Fitting joints to bears, pages 52–55**

NUT AND BOLT JOINTS

These reliable joints have been around for many years; you will find many old bears held together by nuts and bolts, some for as long as 70 years. They are used when making collectors' bears, and are particularly useful when making very large bears as the joints can be made very tight and are often available in larger sizes than other joints. They are also excellent for anyone with limited strength in their hands.

When using nut and bolt joints, position and tighten them *before* the bear is filled. Leave openings in the seams of all the limbs and one side of the head gusset. You can tighten the nuts with wrenches or ratchets, but the easiest way is to use two nut drivers and screw them together.

YOU WILL NEED

To assemble a nut and bolt joint
Bear pieces to be jointed, not filled
Nut and bolt joints of the correct size for the bear you are making
Two nut drivers, or wrench and ratchet
Awl to make holes in the fur fabric, or small pointed scissors

1 With an awl or a pair of small pointed scissors, make a hole in the fabric where the joint stem will go through. Try to separate the threads rather than cut through them.

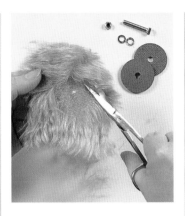

2 | If using long pile fur fabric, trim the area around the hole that the joint is going to cover. This will give a tighter fit.

3 | The area of pile to be cut should be just big enough to be covered by the disk, and no larger, or a bare patch will be noticeable.

4 | Place one metal washer, followed by one hardboard disk onto the bolt. Then push this through the two layers of fabric until it protrudes on the other side. (When this is done from a limb onto the body, it is usually done in two stages: first through the limb, then through the body.)

5 | Place the other hardboard disk followed by the second metal washer onto the protruding bolt. Then start to put the nut in place with your fingers. You will only be able to do a few turns.

6 | Take the nut drivers and put one on each side. Twist them at the same time, but in opposite directions, until the joint is tight. (Alternatively you can use a wrench to hold the head of the bolt in place, and turn the nut with a ratchet.)

7 | Take the nut driver off to see how far down the bolt the nut is. Do not overtighten or the limb will move but not rotate; this can cause the material to tear. If the nut is too tight then undo it slightly. Do this only once or twice to avoid damaging the nylon insert in the nut which enables it to grip the bolt.

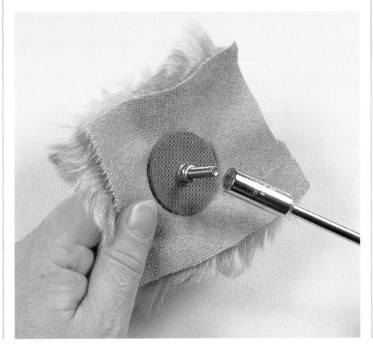

COTTER PIN JOINTS (also called split pins)

These are very traditional and most often used for collectors' bears. Again, they have been used since bears were first made, mainly because there was very little choice of components available and these seemed to do the job very well—they remain as popular today as always. They are also inexpensive and very straightforward to use. When choosing joints, look for the ones with "T" headed pins, as these are less likely to pull through the disk hole. They are easy to tighten, but practice does make perfect.

These joints are usually put in place *after* the limbs and head have been filled, because the joint is tightened by pulling rather than pushing. Openings are usually left on the top of the limbs, and the neck opening is used for fitting the joint in the head. These joints are tightened by using a pair of pliers, or a special cotter key.

YOU WILL NEED

To assemble a cotter pin joint

Bear pieces to be jointed
Cotter pin joints of the right size for the bear to be jointed
Awl or pair of small pointed scissors
Pair of pliers or cotter key

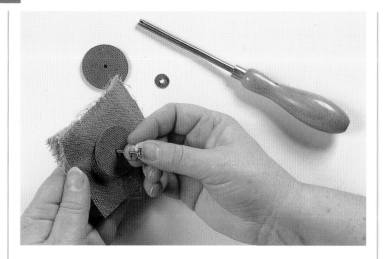

1 Make a hole through the fur with the awl or point of the scissors; you will need a smaller hole than for nut and bolt joints. If you are using long pile fur, trim the fur first, as shown in steps 2–3 of Nut and Bolt Joints. Place one metal washer and one hardboard disk onto the cotter pin. Push this through the two layers of fabric (usually a limb and the body).

2 Place the other hardboard disk and then the other metal washer onto the pin. With your fingers or the pliers, pull the two halves of the pin apart to form a "V" shape.

3 The cotter key is the easier to use of the two tools, but the method is exactly the same if you are using pliers. Place the cotter key (or the pliers) about one quarter of the way down on one side of the split pin and turn it toward the middle. Repeat this for the second side of the split pin, until they form a heart shape.

4 Place the cotter key halfway down each pin and bend them outward until the first bend touches the metal washer.

5 They now form a "crown" shape. As the pin is forced onto the washer, it is pulled up through the middle of the joint, thus making it tight. It is absolutely essential that the bent pin arms both rest on the metal washer, and not just on the hardboard disk, or the joint will not be tight enough. This will also cause wear and tear on the disk, and again this will eventually loosen the joint as the limb is moved.

SAFETY PLASTIC JOINTS

As their name suggests, these are used for bears that are safe for children to play with. There are two main types, both of which are used in the same way. White joints have ridges on the stems with a locking washer that will go past the ridges but will not be able to come back up again. Black joints have a smooth shaft which is gripped by a lock washer; it also cannot move back up the stem. Both types are equally good.

These joints are put in place *before* the bear is filled, because they are pushed together and so both sides must be on a firm base to get a good tight fit. If you press against a filled limb the force will be absorbed and won't make the joint tight. Joints can be tightened by placing a wooden spool or a special safety joint punch onto the stem, over the metal or plastic washer, and tapping the joint firmly with a hammer as far down the stem as possible.

YOU WILL NEED
To assemble safety plastic joints
Bear pieces to be jointed
Safety plastic joints of the size required by the bear
Awl or small pair of small pointed scissors
Wooden spool or safety joint punch
Hammer or mallet

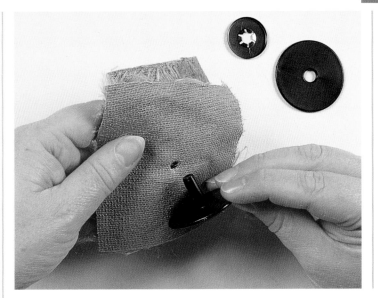

3 Cover the stem with the spool or a joint punch and tap it with a hammer or mallet two or three times. Do this on the floor or on the corner of a firm table for best results.

1 Make a hole in the fabric with the awl or pointed scissors; if using long pile fur fabric, trim it first as shown in steps 2–3 of Nut and Bolt Joints. Push the disk with the stem through the two layers.

2 Place the large disk over the stem and then put the retaining washer on. Press part of the way down with your fingers.

4 The locking washer should be forced as far as possible down the stem to form a tight joint.

SWIVEL NECK JOINT

This is a more recent addition to the range of bear making components. This joint makes it possible to pose the bear in a wider variety of positions, which can add a whole new dimension to its character. It may seem rather daunting at first to fit, but a little patience and perseverance pays off, when you see how expressive the bear looks. It is somewhat more expensive than the other joints, but considering its many different parts and the precision engineering of its manufacture, the expense is justified by the way it increases the appeal of the bear.

YOU WILL NEED
To assemble a swivel neck joint

Bear head and body, not filled
Swivel neck joint of the appropriate size
Needle and very strong thread
Awl or pair of small pointed scissors

1 With the head inside out, and using very strong thread, sew running stitches around the neck edge and gather. Finish off well with several small stitches.

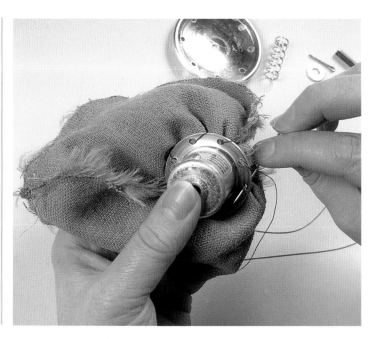

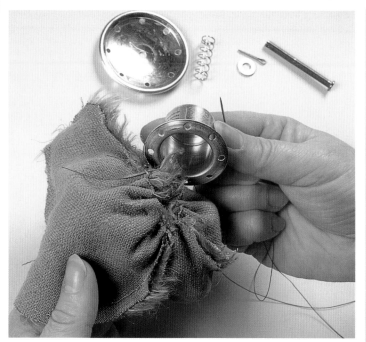

2 Place the "top hat" shaped piece over the opening.

3 Stitch in place by sewing through the holes around the edge.

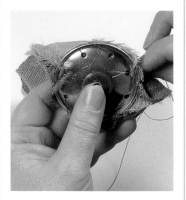

4 With the body inside out, make an opening large enough to accommodate the large disk. Stitch this in place through the holes around the edge of the disk.

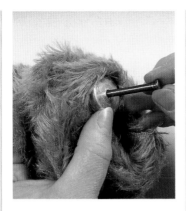

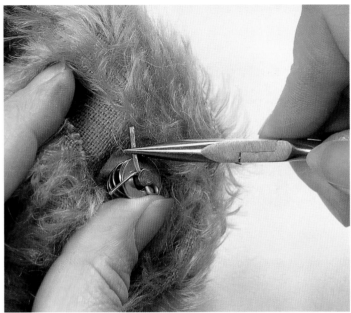

5 Turn the body and head the right way out. Take the long pin and push it through the "top hat" in the head, down through the opening in the middle of the large disk until it appears in the body.

7 Place the metal washer over the pin, and push the small split pin through the hole in the top of the long pin, to hold the spring and washer in place. Take care as the spring is very strong and may cause damage if not held firmly in place before securing.

8 Split the small holding pin open and bend the two sides flat to make sure that it does not come out.

6 Take the spring and put this over the pin and push it down; hold this firmly in place.

Turning and Putting Joints In

When all the bear pieces are stitched, it is time to turn them and put the joints in. The pieces should be turned with care to avoid damaging the fabric. Here the order in which you assemble the joints is extremely important. The type of joint used may also affect the order.

First, make sure that you know where the joints will go. Commercial patterns usually have some points marked to indicate this. They would have been transferred to the back of the fur fabric when you traced the patterns onto the fabric, but check, after stitching, to see if they are evenly placed and that they will fit the recommended size joint. The process of stitching sometimes affects the position of the points, as the fabric may have been pulled more on one side than the other.

If you have used your own pattern, you will have to determine the position of the points yourself. It is important that these are accurate. Do not turn the bear right side out until you have marked all the joint points. These can be transferred to the right side with a pin or a piece of thread of a contrasting color.

JOINTS Choose a joint that fits comfortably in the top part of the limb, with about ¼in around, to allow for the thickness of the disk. The neck and the top of the legs may be wider than the top of the arms, so you may need two different sizes of joints.

☞
Putting joints in the bear, pages 46–7

ASSEMBLING The order of assembly between putting joints in and stuffing varies according to the type of joint that you decide to use. In general it is as follows:

Nut and Bolt Joints: The bear must be empty for these joints to be put in, to allow access for the tools required to close the joint. It is stuffed afterward.
Cotter Pin Joints: Traditionally the head is stuffed first, and a cotter pin joint fitted in the neck. This is then joined to the empty body. It can also be done with the head empty. The arms and legs can be empty or stuffed when the joints are put in.
Safety Plastic Joints: These are best used on an empty bear, as they need to be hammered in place with a special tool.

In all cases the body has to remain empty until all five joints are tightened, and only then can it be filled.

TURNING

We are going to mark the points where the joints will go with the help of the disks of the joints, before turning the bear pieces right side out. Those points are where we will make holes for the bolt, cotter pin, or safety joint stem to go through.

1 Set out all the stitched pieces in "bear" position on the table, to check that nothing is missing.

YOU WILL NEED
For putting joints in and turning
Bear pieces, stitched but not turned
Joints of the correct size for the bear
Pencil or ballpoint pen
Forceps or hemostats and/or stuffing sticks
Fray check liquid or white glue

---

2 Where the curves are sharp, snip the seam allowance with a pair of sharp pointed scissors, to about ¹⁄₁₆in from the stitching, and put a drop of fray check liquid, or white glue, along the raw edge of the fabric.

3 | This is an "X-ray" picture of the joint positions. The joints are shown untightened, for clarity; when properly closed, the disks will be much closer together.

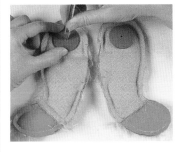

4 | Place the arms inner sides up. Put a disk at the top of each arm, ¼in below the top stitching line. With a pen, mark the fabric through the hole in the disk. Then place the legs, with the feet facing outward so that the inner sides are up, place the disks at the top and mark the joint points as done for the arms.

5 | To mark the leg position, draw an imaginary line centrally on one side of the body, from neck to crotch. In a four-piece body there will be a seam line there already. Take the same disk used for marking the legs, and place it on that line, about ½in up from the lower seam for a medium size bear. This allows for the bear's crotch. If your bear is bigger or smaller, you may need to alter the distance. Mark the point through the hole. In a four-piece body, the mark should go on the body back, next to the seam but not through it.

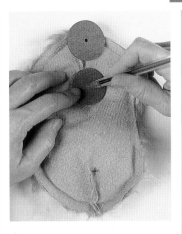

6 | To mark arm position on body, place a disk from the neck joint on the top of the body, the hole on the top seam line. This allows for the neck joint. Place a disk from an arm joint along the central line, approximately ½in below this disc for a medium bear, more or less for bigger or smaller size bears, and mark the point through the hole where the joint will go.

7 | Transfer the marks to the other side of the body, using a colored-headed pin, and/or some colored thread, keeping the body very flat.

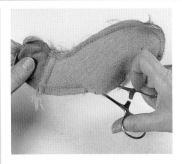

8 | Turn the body pieces. The best tool for long narrow pieces like the arms and legs is a pair of forceps. Put them inside the piece to be turned, and with the forceps' jaws, grab a section of fabric at the other end; the whole fabric, not just the fur fibers.

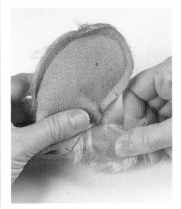

9 | Lock the jaws, and very gently pull the forceps out, sliding and rolling the fabric with your other hand to avoid too much pull on the fabric. When the end is out, remove the forceps and finish turning the piece with your fingers. Use the locked forceps or a blunt stuffing stick to push out the seams from inside the pieces.

INSERTING JOINTS

When all the points are marked, use an awl or the point of a pair of scissors to make the holes for the joints. Place the disk with the cotter pin, the bolt, or the plastic stem through the hole, from the inside of the limb to the outside.

YOU WILL NEED

Putting joints in the bear
Bear pieces, unfilled
Stiff wire brush
Joints of the right size
Awl
Sharp pointed scissors
Long thick needle
Strong thread
Appropriate tools for
    closing the joints

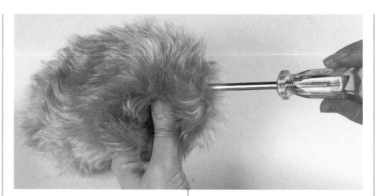

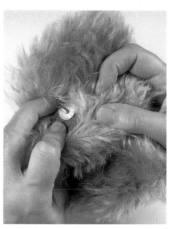

2 First put the joint in the head. This is shown on an empty head, but it can be done in a filled head if you are using cotter pin joints. With a large needle and strong thread sew a row of gathering stitches ¼in from the edge of the neck.

4 Make a hole in the top of the body, near the central line, next to the stitching. The precise spot you choose depends on the effect you want to create— a bear with the head tilted upward, or downward, or straight.

5 Push the pin from the head into this hole, and inside the body; slip the other disk and washer through, and close it as shown on page 47.

1 At this stage you should look at the seams from the outside, and if a lot of fur fibers are caught in the stitching, release them by rubbing and picking with a long thick needle, and brushing with a stiff wire brush.

3 Place the half joint with the washer and disk inside the neck and the pin, bolt, or stem sticking out. Pull the gathers tightly, and close securely. Trim the hair in the joint area, so the joint closure can be made tighter.

☞
Putting joints in the bear, pages 46–51

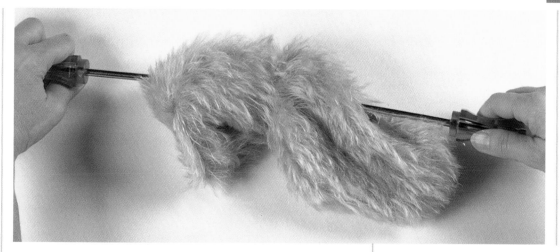

9 One variation is to make bendable limbs by using a piece of plastic-covered wire inside a foam sleeve. This can be fitted in conjunction with a bolt joint inside the legs and/or arms. Attach the top of this flexible stem to the bolt and disk through its special attachment, and bend the lower end to fit the foot. This can be cut shorter if necessary.

6 If you are using nut and bolt joints, you must have an empty head with an opening in one of the gusset seams, so you can use the tools to tighten the joint from both sides.

7 For the arms and legs, turn back the appropriate area of each piece, and make the hole for the joint using the awl or the point of a pair of scissors. Do this for all four limbs and the body.

8 From the inside of the arms and the legs, slip cotter pin, bolt, or stem through the hole, so it sticks out on the outside. Do this for all four limbs.

10 Insert the flexible stem into the leg, and put the bolt through the prepared hole as usual.

11 The leg is stuffed *after* the bolt is attached to the body.

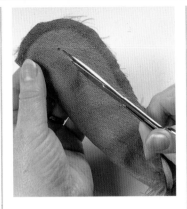

12 Another variation is to stitch the arms and legs without leaving any opening at all. To turn the limb, cut a slit lengthwise in the inner limb with sharp scissors, so that the point of the joint sits in the middle of the line.

14 Stuff the limb with your chosen filling before putting the half joint in.

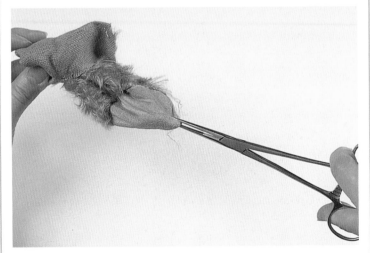

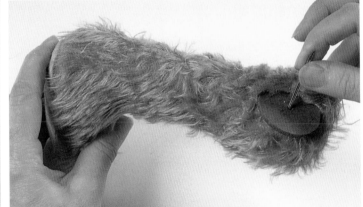

15 Place the joint into the arm through the slit. Only cotter pin joints can be used effectively with this method.

13 Carefully use a pair of forceps to turn the limb right side out.

16 Oversew the slit with strong thread and needle. The raw edges and the stitching are hidden under the limb after the joints have been put in the bear.

ASSEMBLING

The bear is ready to be assembled. The points of the joint in the body have to be checked again, and the joints tightened securely.

1 Place the pieces out in "bear" shape, to make sure all the pieces have had their joints put in correctly, and the bear has left and right arms and legs. Check that all the pieces of the second half of the joints are there too.

2 Make the holes in the points marked on the body, and slip the pins from the leg joints through them. Check the feet face forward and that both legs reach the floor evenly when standing. If not, adjust the holes.

3 Carefully seat the bear, so you can see if the back of the legs are even with the bottom. Adjust if necessary. Close and tighten the joints from inside the body.

4 Fit the arms through the body holes in the same way as for the legs. Check that there is a proper shoulder, and that the bear does not look "hunched." When you are satisfied, close the joints and and tighten them.

5 All the joints of the bear have now been completed. As it is most likely empty, and has no features, it may look rather strange. But it is quickly taking shape. The next step is to stuff it.

Stuffing the Bear

The way you stuff your bear adds to its character, and it is another way that you can put your artistic talents to good use. Consider the bear you are making and choose the right filling from the range available, according to the effect you want to produce. Always buy good quality filling; it is as important, if not more important, than the fabric you choose, as many a bear has been ruined by poor quality stuffing.

Many different types of bear stuffing are available, such as polyester, plastic pellets, wood wool, and Kapok. In addition, steel shot is often used in miniature bears. Improvised fillings such as old pantyhose or cotton are not really recommended.

The filling you choose depends very much on the type of bear you are making. Traditionalists prefer wood wool and Kapok, while pellets and polyester are used more for modern bears and children's bears. Bears filled with fine glass beads are a recent innovation, but they should be used as ornaments only and should be clearly labeled. If you use glass beads, handle them with care as they are smaller than sand particles. Always wear a mask to avoid inhaling them accidentally and use gloves to prevent them getting under your finger nails. If you do ingest any accidentally, you should seek medical attention immediately.

Different styles may be achieved by mixing different fillings. For instance, wood wool and polyester are particularly good when "teased" together.

☞
Safety, pages 8–9

STUFFING WITH POLYESTER FILLING

Many types of polyester filling are available, so choose carefully. Most of the filling sold is called "High Loft" or "fluffy." Although an excellent filling, the fibers have been crimped to make the filling very light and bouncy, and it is used mainly for making stuffed toys and children's toy bears. The other type of filling is untreated and it remains very flat and heavy, which is ideal for filling a bear very firmly. Make sure you use a good quality filling and not a by-product or factory scraps.

YOU WILL NEED
For stuffing the bear
Polyester filling
Stuffing stick
Stiff wire brush
Bear ready to be filled

1 Tease the filling out a little at a time to check for lumps. For best results, pack small amounts of filling into the bear a little at a time. Do not attempt to put too much in at one time as this can make it lumpy.

2 Push the filling in with a stuffing stick, which enables you to reach small channels that your fingers would not and to push the filling harder. It is possible to improvise and use things such as a wooden spoon handle, but avoid sharp tools such as knitting needles or chopsticks as these can cause damage. Using the right tool for the job does make it a lot easier.

3 Pack from the furthest corner out toward the opening, feeling the bear from the outside to make sure that there are no empty places or wrinkles in the fabric. Brush pile away from the opening in order to sew it together.

CLOSING THE OPENINGS: USING A LADDER STITCH

Ladder stitch is possibly the most important stitch that you will need when making a bear. It is an invisible stitch that enables you to close the gaps left by filling or putting joints in, so that they look like a continuation of the seams. Because the stitch is hidden, the color of thread used does not matter very much. If the thread shows, then what you are doing is not really a ladder stitch. It is important, to use a *very* strong thread as it has to be pulled very tightly.

YOU WILL NEED

To close the openings
Extra strong thread
Sewing needle
Scissors
Stiff wire brush
Bear to be sewn

1 Turn the edge of the opening back and take three or four small stitches in the seam allowance, making sure that the stitches do not show on the right side at all. Push the needle out through the seam to the right side just at the start of the opening.

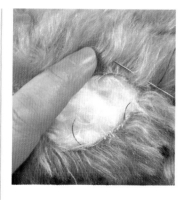

2 Working from right to left take a small stitch parallel to the seam in the top edge, about the same distance from the edge as the seam allowance, about ¼in

3 The second stitch should be opposite the first on the other side, at the same distance from the edge (¼in) and still parallel to the seam.

4 Keep taking stitches one above the other on one side and then the other. If done correctly the stitches will form bars, like rungs on a ladder—hence the name.

5 While squeezing the edges together, pull the thread tight until the stitches disappear. You will find this easier if you do it after every two or three stitches.

6 You will find that the raw edges automatically turn under leaving a smooth finish. The colored-headed pin indicates where the seam ended and the ladder stitch began. Continue stitching to the end of the opening.

7 Bring the needle out into the seam and take a few tiny back stitches.

8 Then put the needle in and bring it out about two inches away before cutting the end. This will give you a secure finish and make sure that the last ladder stitch cannot start to unravel.

PLASTIC PELLETS

Plastic pellets are a wonderful modern filling. Although not strictly traditional, they are widely used in modern collectors' bears. They may be put directly into the bear's cavities, however, if you wish to use them for a child's bear, then they must be protected and placed first inside a thin cotton bag. They not only add weight, but can also completely alter the style and feel of your bear. If filled loosely, they can achieve a very floppy cuddly look; if packed tightly, they result in a solid and very weighty bear. These pellets are, in fact, the raw material used for injection molding. Try to find pellets that are small, about the size of a grain of rice, nicely rounded, and that do not smell of plastic, as this will affect your finished bear.

YOU WILL NEED
For filling with pellets
Plastic pellets
Kapok or polyester filling
Stuffing stick
Small tube
Funnel
Scoop

1 | Usually pellets are only put in the body and limbs; they do not look particularly attractive used in the head. Start by packing the shoulder area of your bear's body with soft filling. This will help support the head a little so that it doesn't sag too much. Pack the bottom area to help with support as well.

2 | Pellets have a tendency to spread everywhere, so it is better if they can be kept under control. If filling a small bear, use a small candy tube. This may be pushed right into the bear and the pellets placed at the bottom. Work your way toward the opening in the back seam.

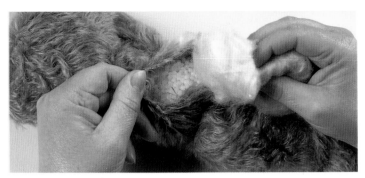

3 | Before attempting the ladder stitch, cover the pellets with a small pad of filling. This will prevent them from bouncing out when pulling the edges together.

4 | When filling the limbs, pack the pad area with soft filling first. Pads don't look or feel as nice if the pellets can be felt; they can also cause more wear and tear, especially on fine fabrics. Another method for putting pellets in is to use a scoop and funnel.

5 | Again, put a small pad over the last pellets to keep them in place when sewing the opening closed.

STUFFING WITH WOOD WOOL

Wood wool is exactly what the name suggests—long fine strands of wood tangled up, with the appearance of wool. It makes an excellent filling because it can be packed really firmly. This material is widely used nowadays to make true replicas or traditional bears. Many makers of collectable bears prefer to use these old fashioned fillings. However, they are completely unsuitable for use in children's bears because of their high fire risk. Any part of the bear may be filled with this stuffing, but it is especially good to use in the head as it makes putting in glass eyes and embroidering noses much easier.

YOU WILL NEED
For filling with wood wool
Wood wool
Stuffing stick
Bear to be filled

1 Choose a good quality fine grade wood wool. Keep it moist but not wet; don't let it dry out too much. If it becomes brittle, spray lightly with water. Keep it in a cool dark place in a plastic bag with holes for ventilation.

3 With your fingers, push this into your bear, molding it to the desired shape. For long limbs and large bodies you may find the special wood wool stuffing stick useful.

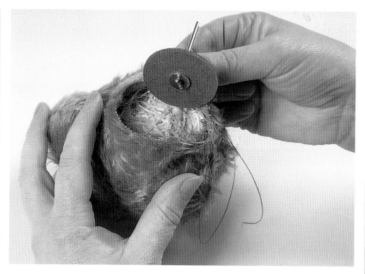

2 Pull out a little at a time and check for coarse pieces as you pull it. Roll a small amount in the palm of your hand until you form a small ball.

4 Fill your bear toward the opening packing it tightly, feeling the outside of your bear for any lumps or soft areas. Leave the last piece smooth for the joint to sit nicely in place.

STUFFING WITH KAPOK

Kapok comes from a seed pod. It is the soft layer under the husk that protects the seeds. This is another natural product that was very popular in old bears because it was cheap and readily available. Kapok is very fibrous and made up of millions of minuscule particles, so it is very important to keep it under control. It is so light that it will soon fill the air so don't take too much out at once. If handled correctly it can make an excellent filling and really enhance your collectors' bears.

YOU WILL NEED
Stuffing with Kapok
Kapok
Stuffing stick
Bear to be filled

When handling Kapok, it is prudent to wear a mask, especially if you suffer from asthma.

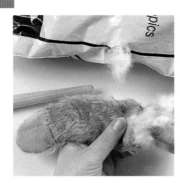

1 When you start a new bag of filling, never tear the top open. There will be a few breathing holes in the bag; enlarge one of these with a finger until you are able to pinch a small amount between finger and thumb and pull it out gently. Using small amounts, pack the Kapok into your bear very firmly, checking as you do so for empty spaces or lumps.

2 The use of a stuffing stick will help to produce a very firm finish. Don't try to push too much in at any one time. Work your way toward the opening and finish in the same way as for the other fillings.

FITTING GROWLERS AND MUSICAL MOVEMENTS

Many bear makers fit a voice box into their bears to add another dimension, and they are a lot of fun. Children's bears particularly lend themselves to the delights of the growler. When choosing a growler, check that it will fit your bear so that no edges may be felt when in place. Musical movements should be of good quality with a sturdy case and attractive key.

YOU WILL NEED
To fit a growler or musical movement
Bear, partly filled
Growler or musical box
Extra strong thread
Needle
Scissors

1 Partly fill the body of the bear with either Kapok or polyester filling. Leave a cavity the size of the growler to be fitted. The growler should be placed inside the bear horizontally. If the perforations face the front the bear will growl when tipped away from you; if the perforations are at the back, it will growl when tilted toward you. If the growler is upright, the bear will have to stand on its head to make it growl.

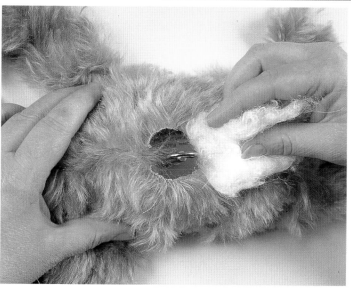

2 Pack the filling around the growler until it is held firmly in place with no gaps, then cover it with a pad of filling on the top to protect it before closing the opening with a ladder stitch.

4 Pack the filling firmly around the box and pad the top around the key to cover any edges.

5 Sew the edges together around the key using a ladder stitch so that it is held firmly in place.

3 Put the musical movement in in exactly the same way as the growler. Form the cavity first, and then place the box inside so that the key is protruding from the back seam.

Teddy bear features

Putting the heart and soul into your bear: creating its expression through the eyes, nose, mouth and ears, so it can communicate with the world.

Eyes

They say that the eyes are the windows of the soul. This is very true in humans but it can also be said of the humble Teddy Bear. More than anything, the eyes give your bear its character and reflect exactly what mood it is in. A well made bear is one that when looked at will look right back at you. Use your artistry when you choose the color and size of the eyes; it is all important in achieving exactly the right expression for your bear.

When the first bears were made there was very little choice of what you could use for Teddy Bears' eyes. In fact a lot of bears had black shoe buttons for eyes. Today these are simulated, as real shoe buttons are few and far between, but they did the job so well that they are still popular today. Later, eyes were made out of glass, usually amber in color or just plain crystal. In the late fifties and early sixties new legislation banned the use of potentially dangerous components in the making of bears. For many years bears were made as toys in man-made fabrics with plastic eyes and joints and the traditional bears started to disappear. Nowadays if bears are made with glass eyes they are labeled as being suitable for collectors only. It is due to the resurgence of the popularity of the traditional bears that manufacturers now produce a wonderful range of glass eyes to choose from. They come in all sizes from tiny ⅟₂₅in black eyes to giant 1¼in eyes for huge bears. The solid black glass are by far the most popular in all sizes, but there

are also painted enameled eyes in a variety of colors and glass eyes with a black pupil in an array of dazzling hues. Of course, bears for children are still made using plastic safety eyes, so the range may not be as varied but they are still available in a large range of sizes and in traditional Teddy colors.

The eyes are fitted in various ways, depending on the type used. Glass eyes come either pre-looped, or on wires, and plastic eyes have safety washers to secure them. Since the position of the eyes can change the whole expression of your bear, this together with the infinite combinations of color and size make it the single most important choice in the making of your bear.

PREPARING GLASS EYES ON WIRES
Many of the glass eyes are available already pre-looped. Some though, because of the way they are made, have to be produced on wires. These are often a little cheaper and will provide a greater variety to choose from when deciding on how to finish your bear. It is not difficult to make your own loops but care should be taken as they are fragile and should be handled gently.

> **Positioning, color, and size of eyes— examples in the Gallery, pages 120–47**

YOU WILL NEED
To prepare glass eyes on wires
One pair of glass eyes on wires the correct size and color
Pair of pliers
Wire cutters (if the pliers do not have a wire cutter included)

1 One pair of eyes will be on one wire; these must be separated by cutting with wire cutters. Many pairs of pliers will have this extra facility.

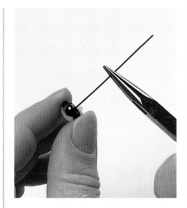

2 | Holding the eye gently with one hand place the pliers about halfway along the wire.

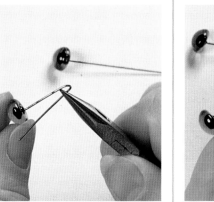

3 | Bend the wire over toward you to form a "U" shape.

4 | Hold the wire with the pliers and use your other hand to twist the end of the wire around itself. Do not hold the glass eye while doing this.

5 | Keep turning the wire until it is all coiled around. Do not take it too far up the wire toward the eye. Leave about ¼in between the last turn and the glass. If it does touch then this can cause pressure and the eye may pop off.

6 | There will be a sharp end sticking out. Very carefully tuck this in behind the loop with the pliers. If the loop is too large just squash it to form an oval as it only needs to be large enough to push the thread through.

SEWING IN GLASS EYES — BASIC METHOD

Glass eyes are sewn into the bear's head using very strong thread. It is the pulling on the eyes when they are put in that helps to shape the face and make them look as if they belong and are not just stuck on. Traditionally the eyes are sewn into the back of the head where the stitches and inevitable dimple will be hidden. There are alternative positions which will be explained in this section. Positioning is the most important part of putting the eyes in. All eyes on humans are level with the bridge of the nose, which is why when eyes are set too wide or too high on a bear they look "wrong," because we automatically relate better to the norm. The position on this line, the bridge, is a matter of personal preference; some eyes are placed very close together on the actual gusset while others are on the side head pieces. It is this sort of decision that brings out your artistry and the individuality of the bear.

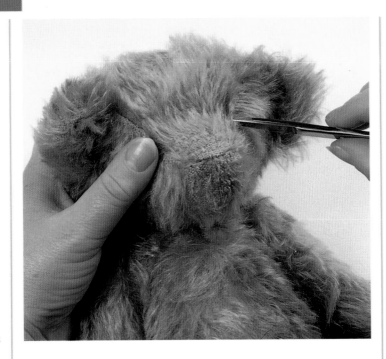

1 Find the position where you want the eyes by pushing the nose up slightly; this makes a crease, which is at the level that the eyes should be. Put thumb tacks in to make absolutely sure that the position is correct. Look from all angles to check. Make the required holes in the head of your bear with a sharp instrument. Be sure to make the hole big enough to accommodate long shanks, but not so wide as to be able to pull the eye through the backing. If you are unsure about which color or size of eye to choose then try different ones at this stage.

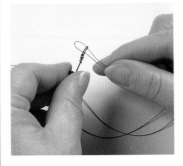

2 Take a long piece of very strong thread and fold it in half. Pass this loop through the wire loop on the eye.

3 Take the two ends and pass those through the loop in the thread, pull tight. This attaches the thread to the eye and cannot come undone.

4 Use a needle that is long enough to go through the head comfortably and that can be held firmly at both ends. Thread the needle with the thread that is attached to the eye. Push the needle into the head through the hole that you made for the eye until it appears at the base of the head at the back. Pull the needle all the way through and remove, leaving the two ends of thread hanging down. Pull those ends until the eye fits into the head.

YOU WILL NEED

To sew glass eyes
Extra strong thread
Long needle
Sharp scissors or an awl
Glass eyes, looped, of the
    right color and size
Bear's head, filled
Ordinary sewing needle

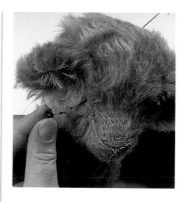

5 | Do the same with the other eye, making sure that the needle comes out adjacent to the other threads at the back of the head, but not in exactly the same place. Make sure that when you pull the threads the eyes can move freely. When you hold the thread in one hand and the eye in the other and pull back and forth there should be no obstruction.

6 | Turn the bear over and tie a knot with the two double threads.

7 | Turn the bear back again and put your thumbs over the eyes. Push very firmly while pulling on the threads on the other side. This takes the pressure off the glass while still making sure that the eyes are pulled in very tightly. Tie several knots on top of the first, making sure that they do not become loose.

8 | Using a normal sized needle, thread two of the four thread tails, insert the needle close to the knot, and bring it out again in the head gusset seam. Take a few small back stitches then bring the needle out about two inches away before cutting off. Repeat with the other two threads. If you don't do this, and cut the ends after knotting, then the knots may come undone and the eyes will work loose.

SEWING IN GLASS EYES— ALTERNATIVE METHODS

If you choose a very short pile fabric, you will not always want the "dimple" at the back of the head because it shows more. If you use a firm filling in a large head, it may be difficult to put the needle through. Or you may not have a needle long enough for a large head. In these cases, finding an alternative place for sewing the eyes is preferable.

1 | Finishing under the chin
Follow steps 1–4 of the basic method but push the needle down in the direction of the base of the neck at the front. Do the other eye in exactly the same way.

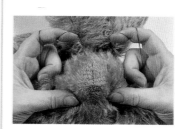

2 | Tie the ends together and while pulling tight, push on the eyes to make sure they go in tightly. To finish follow step 8, but do your back stitches right down at the neck edge where they won't be seen.

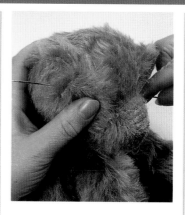

1 | Finishing behind the ear
Follow steps 1–4 of the basic method but when you push the needle in for the first eye bring it out behind the ear diagonally opposite. Do the same with the second eye.

2 | There will be two threads protruding from behind the ear. Take a small stitch with one of them to separate them. Tie these two together very tightly while pushing on the eye. Then sew the ends in as before, taking small back stitches behind the ear so that they won't be seen. Repeat for the second eye.

PAINTING GLASS EYES

With all the wonderful array of colored fur fabrics on the market today, it is sometimes difficult to find just the right shade of eye color to complement your bear. One way of overcoming this problem is to color the eyes yourself. Using clear crystal glass eyes and acrylic-based paints, it is an easy, yet satisfying solution.

YOU WILL NEED

For coloring eyes

Crystal glass eyes of
 appropriate size
Acrylic paints
Paintbrush
Palette
Mixing spatula
Pliers to hold eyes if not
 on wires

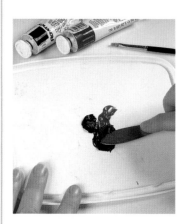

1 Use the paint straight from the tube, either as it is or mix two or three colors together until you find the desired shade.

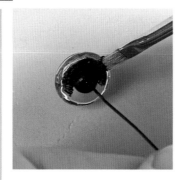

2 It is easier if the eyes are on wires, but if there are loops, just hold them with a pair of pliers while you paint. Use a fine brush and start at the middle and work your way out to the edge, turning the eye as you go.

3 Turn the eye over to face you and brush from the inside toward the outer edge to make sure that the whole area is covered. Place the eyes somewhere safe to dry. When completely dry attach them to your bear in exactly the same way as other glass eyes.

FABRIC BACKINGS FOR GLASS EYES

If your eyes are *almost* the right color, but need to be made darker, a good way of doing this is to back them with a small piece of fabric. It is best to use a non-fraying fabric, such as felt or Ultrasuede, in a darker color than the eye, but not necessarily in the same shade; for example, a dark brown fabric will make lavender eyes look a deeper purple.

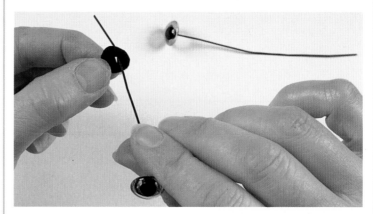

1 Cut two circles of fabric the same size but in a darker color than the eyes. Make a tiny snip in the center of the circle with sharp scissors (the hole may have to be bigger if using pre-looped eyes). Slip the wire or loop of the eye through the hole.

YOU WILL NEED

For fabric backing

Fairly dark, non-fraying
 fabric
Pair of light-colored glass
 eyes
Small sharp scissors

2 Check that the fabric does not show outside the rim of the eye. Notice how much darker the eye with the backing looks. The backing will be held in place when the eyes are fitted to the bear.

SAFETY EYES

Safety plastic eyes are used when making a bear for a child. The components used must comply to the safety standards of the country. The eyes are held by either a lock washer or a plastic washer being pushed onto the back of the eye. To do this you need to have access to both sides of the eye when fitting. If the position is marked and a hole made when the head is empty, then it is very difficult to be accurate and very often the eyes look a little crooked. To overcome this and to insure a tight fit, follow the method shown below.

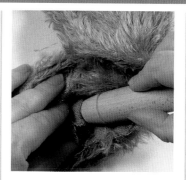

YOU WILL NEED
For fitting safety eyes
Safety eyes of the appropriate color and size
Unfilled bear's head
Filling that complies with safety requirements
Awl or pointed scissors
Joint punch or spool of thread

3 | At this point try different colors and sizes of eye in the holes until you find the one that looks the best. Then remove the filling.

5 | Using a joint punch or a spool, push the washer firmly in place as far down the stem as it will go. The head may now be filled and the eyes will be correctly placed.

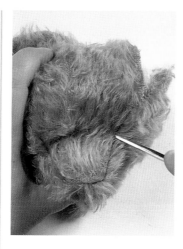

1 | Fill the empty bear's head firmly with your chosen filling, making sure that the muzzle is well filled and that the filling is not loose.

2 | To find the position of where to make the eye hole, push the bear's nose up slightly to find the bridge of the nose, in the same way as explained for glass eyes. Make the hole at the point where the bridge meets the side gusset seam using sharp scissors or an awl. Do not make the hole too big—it is better to part the threads rather than cut them. With safety eyes particularly, there must not be any risk of their being pulled out once fixed.

4 | Push the eyes into the head from the right side so that the stem is on the inside of the head. Put a metal or plastic washer onto the back of the eyes to secure them in place.

Noses

Traditional bear noses are embroidered. They are sewn in a variety of shapes and sizes, usually black or brown, but there are no definite rules. You may choose colors to complement the mohair, or even make them multi-colored. The only limit is your imagination, and it should be great fun designing your bear's nose.

It has been said that it takes two days to make a bear and another two days to embroider the nose. This should not put you off doing the traditional nose, rather just make you aware that it takes time and practice. It is important to have the right tools for the job: without sharp needles and good quality thread, producing a good embroidered nose is more difficult.

The stitch used is a simple satin stitch; long, straight stitches very close to each other, so the area is completely covered and the fabric underneath is not visible. To achieve this, it is best to trim the fur from the area to be embroidered, or even to pluck it out altogether.

THE MUZZLE You can create a variety of different looks by shaving the muzzle—either large parts or the whole thing. Skillful trimming allows you to sculpt the features and to indicate the age and sex of your bear. You may also want to experiment with other materials, as shown with the leather nose in this section.

The foundations are all important, and the muzzle area must be packed very tightly with good quality filling. The best choice for the nose is wood wool , but if you do not wish to use it to fill the whole head, it is possible to fill just the muzzle area with wood wool, and to use polyester stuffing for the rest of the head. The seams must be accurate. If the starting point is right then the nose will be much easier to do. (See Inserting the head gusset, pages 36–7.)

TRIMMING THE MUZZLE

Many people are wary of cutting the fur, but if done slowly and carefully it can only enhance your bear. Use very sharp and pointed scissors. Trim very small amounts at a time, and keep changing the angle of the scissors to avoid straight lines. Start at the top and work down a little at a time, doing the whole area to be trimmed at each stage so that you can stop when you like. If you cut too deep to begin with then it cannot be altered later. Alternatively, the hairs can be plucked for a completely bare look, similar to that of really old Teddies.

YOU WILL NEED
For trimming the muzzle
Sharp pointed scissors for trimming fur
Forceps for plucking fur
Filled bear head

1 Sharp pointed scissors are the best tool if you want to trim only the area where the nose will actually be embroidered. Just cut as far down to the backing as you can, evenly, making sure that there are no long pieces of pile sticking out through the embroidery. Use forceps for plucking to give a better finish and to make sure that all the pile is taken away.

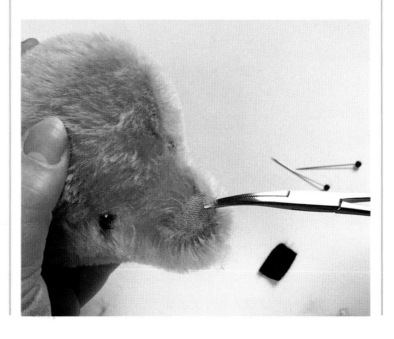

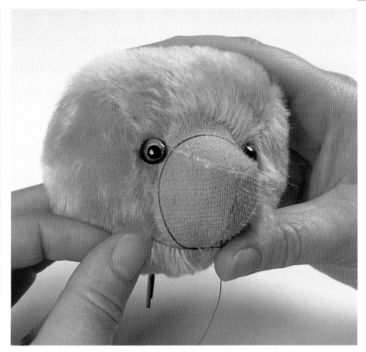

4 If you then remove the pile from the sides, this will give a neat clean finish that shows the eyes off at their best. Place a piece of thread around the muzzle so that you can see if the trimming is even; when you take this much away, it must be accurate.

2 When removing the pile with the forceps, don't try to take too much at once. Hold the bear firmly and pluck the pile out a little at a time. Make sure that you don't pull the backing and make a hole; smooth the backing flat before clamping the pile. Some bears have just the top of the muzzle trimmed, leaving the sides untouched.

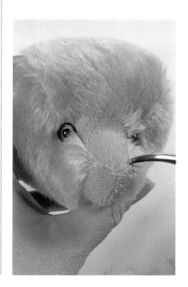

3 This may be continued under the chin to create the "mutton chop" effect. The most important part of trimming the muzzle is in fact the foundation: make absolutely sure that the seam joining the two side head pieces is exactly in the middle of your head gusset when you sew them together. Any discrepancy will show as soon as the pile is removed.

EMBROIDERING THE NOSE

When embroidering the nose on your bear, sew long stitches either horizontally or vertically. First define the area, and then fill it in. Once the area is covered, then the layers may be built up to form the "body." There is no need to do just one layer; as the stitches go one on top of another, any discrepancies can be ironed out. If, at the end, the top edge looks a little ragged, don't despair; it can be given a sharp and professional finish.

YOU WILL NEED

To embroider the nose
Filled bear head
Embroidery thread, usually cotton perle, in black or brown
Soft sculpture needle (bought in doll store), with big eye to hold thick thread
Sharp pointed scissors
Colored-headed pins
Nose templates made in black paper or felt

Traditional

Steiff bear-style

Contemporary style

Elongated style

1 First decide on the size and shape of the nose. Cut out various shapes in black paper or felt, and then pin them to your bear using colored-headed pins until you find the one that looks right. Trim the muzzle as explained in the previous section.

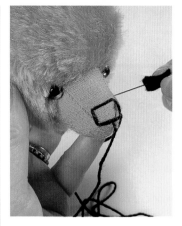

2 Thread the needle and push it in at the side of the muzzle, until it protrudes at the point where the seam at the side head pieces meets the middle of the head gusset. With the template in place, sew stitches around to mark the desired area. Finish with the thread coming out at the middle seam again. Remove the template.

3 Put the needle in at the top edge, and bring it out adjacent to the first thread. Do not pull the thread too tight—just lay it in place and pull until it lies flat. Keep making stitches, within the borders, next to one another across the nose until one half is filled in.

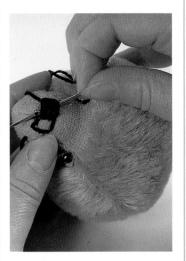

4 When the last stitch is in place, bring the needle out at the middle point again.

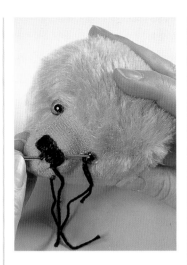

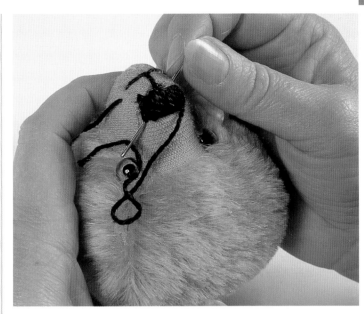

7 If, when you finish the nose, the top edge is a little ragged, sew a long stitch across the top, either before or after sewing the mouth.

5 Fill the other half in the same way making sure that the stitches are not pulled too tight, as this may cause the thread to loop. Again, finish at the middle, ready to do the mouth.

6 If you want points on either side of the nose then just sew large stitches from top to bottom finishing on the midline again.

LEATHER NOSES

Although most noses are traditionally embroidered, it is nice to have an alternative now and then. Noses made in fine leather look very appealing, with a slight shine and a rounded shape. These are easier done on larger bears, as the technique used is rather difficult to do on a small scale. The mouth may be done before or after in the usual way. (See Mouths, pages 78–9.)

YOU WILL NEED

For the nose

Fine glove leather
Templates made in black paper or black felt
Sharp pointed scissors
Needle for sewing leather
Extra strong thread
Pins
Wisp of polyester filling
Forceps

1 Choose the shape and style of the nose by trying different templates, just as for the embroidered nose.

2 Cut the leather a little larger than the template and affix in place with two small pins.

3 Using the extra strong thread and the needle, take a few securing stitches where they won't be seen, just under the nose. Then start to sew around the nose with tiny ladder stitches, first in the leather and then in the fabric.

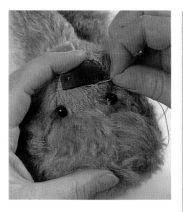

4 The stitches should be about ⅛in in from the edge of the leather, so that when you pull it tight the edge turns under and leaves it even. Remove the pins as you go. Sew all the way around the leather until there is just a small opening left.

5 Using the forceps, fill the nose with a little stuffing. Make it nice and rounded, but do not overfill.

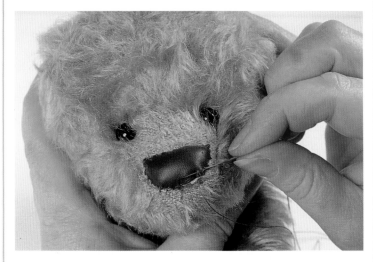

6 Finish sewing around until both ends meet. Take a few tiny back stitches, put the needle in and out again about two inches away, and then cut the thread.

SAFE NOSES

The embroidered nose is safe for children, as long as it is securely stitched following the instructions. Being so attractive, and capable of being made in such a range of different shapes, it is the most likely nose to be used for any bear. There are also safety plastic noses available which are secured with washers in exactly the same way as the safety plastic eyes. However, although plastic eyes, once fitted, are more difficult to tell apart from glass eyes, the plastic safety nose is so obviously different from the traditional embroidered or leather one that it is seldom used. If you want to use one, it is best covered in leather for a more attractive look. (See Fixing safety eyes, page 71.)

YOU WILL NEED

For the safe nose
Safety plastic nose, triangular shape
Small piece of fine glove leather in black or brown
Needle for sewing leather
Strong thread

☞

Fixing safety plastic eyes, page 71

1 Make a template out of paper, following the general shape of the plastic nose, plus ½in all around. Cut the piece in fine glove leather. On the more pointed end, make two folds facing the center, as shown. Overlap them on the lower edge, and coming from behind with the leather needle and strong thread, take a couple of stitches to secure the fold and make the shape of the nose.

2 Using the same needle and strong thread, run a gathering stitch all around the nose cover piece, about ⅛in from the edge, making sure the folded shape stays in place. Pull the gathers slightly.

3 Place the triangular plastic nose inside the leather cover piece, with its pointed triangular end matching the bottom edge of the fold. Pull the gathers tightly around the stem of the nose. Make several stitches across the gathered edges, from one side to the other, knotting and back stitching several times until it feels secure. Snip the thread off.

4 The nose now looks more like a bear's nose and less like a piece of plastic. Fit it on the bear following the instructions for fitting plastic eyes, except that the correct place for the nose is the center of the gusset end, just above where it meets the side-head seams.

Mouths

The mouth gives the bear expression, enhancing the look already defined by the eyes and nose. It uses the very simple technique of making large stitches in the desired shape. The bear may look happy or sad, friendly or upset, just depending on the angle of the stitches used for the mouth.

There are two main styles of mouth: the first is the popular "anchor" style, and the second is made with just two stitches that form an inverted "V" from the midline of the head gusset. You can alter the expression of your bear simply by varying the length and angle of your stitches, as shown below. For example, you could create an "unhappy" expression with a line of straight stitches. Many bear makers like to experiment with the mouth shape to give a unique "characterful" expression, as shown below.

Inverted "V"	Unhappy	Smiling ("anchor")	Characterful variation

STITCHING THE MOUTH

The inverted "V" style is useful if the seam of the head side pieces is not exactly in the middle. If you cover the seam with one thread and then do the other side equidistant from the midline, this gives a neat finish instead of accentuating the discrepancy.

YOU WILL NEED
For the mouth
Colored-headed pins
Soft sculpture needle (bought in doll store)
Embroidery thread: continuation of the nose thread

1 To decide the exact size and style of the mouth, place three colored-headed pins on the muzzle as shown: one on the mid-seam, just below the nose, and one on either side at equal distances from the midline. Wind the thread around the pins to visualize how the mouth will look. If the mouth is too narrow or too wide, just move the pins until the right expression appears.

2 The relationship of the three pins to one another will determine the style. As you can see, if the two side pins are higher than the middle pin then it creates a smile. If they are very much lower then the bear will look grumpy. A balance between the two is preferable.

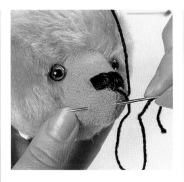

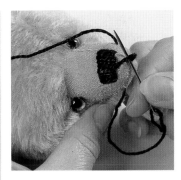

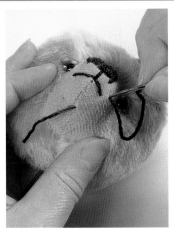

3 | Use the thread from the mid-point of the nose, put the needle in at the middle pin and bring it out at the side by one of the other pins. Do not pull too tightly.

4 | Slip the needle under the bar created by the first stitch, then pull the thread tight, easing the thread as you pull; the tighter you pull, the more the thread will press against the fabric.

6 | If the muzzle is completely bare as shown, then push the needle in again but in exactly the same place—do not make a stitch. If the pile is long, then a tiny stitch will not show. Bring the needle out under the chin. These two stages insure that there is a long enough thread from the final stitch of the mouth so that it is harder to come undone after cutting. Pull the thread tight and then cut. This will make the end spring back into the muzzle.

7 | Re-thread the original end protruding from the side of the muzzle that was left at the beginning of doing the nose. Push the needle in at exactly the same place, so that a stitch is not formed, and out again under the chin. Pull tightly and then cut.

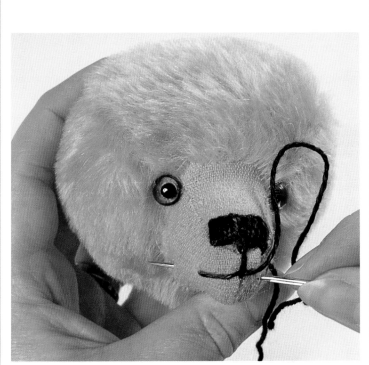

5 | Put the needle in at the position of the second side pin, and out again at the side of the muzzle.

Ears

Ears are a very important feature in a bear. Their

size, position, and curvature can

fundamentally influence its facial

expression. They work in

unison with the eyes, nose,

and mouth as determining traits

of the bear's personality.

Ears have a basic "D" shape, rotated so that they rest on their flat side, and with the curved side on top. The pile always runs up from the flat side toward the curved side. It is particularly important to tease out any hairs caught in the curved seam, and to carefully brush them.

Ears are most often bent into a curved shape, the concave side facing forward, the convex side toward the back. So-called "jug-handle" ears are bigger and flatter, and their shape is created by gathering the lower edge. In other cases, ears may be bent into an "L" shape and one half is stitched to the gusset seamline, and the other side to the head at a right angle.

POSITIONING THE EARS The ears are placed on the top of the head, either straddling across the gusset seams by different amounts, or on the sides, just touching the gusset seams. As the gussets can be of different widths, there is no absolute ratio required between the two features. Try to test different positions until the most pleasing result is achieved.

☞
**Cutting and stitching the
ears, page 39
Ladder stitch, page 59
Needles and threads,
page 10**

STITCHING THE EARS
The ears are often the "handles" of the bear, so stitch them on firmly with extra strong thread, doubled, and always anchor the beginning and end points securely. Use a curved needle to get into the head and the concave side of the ear. Ladder stitch is used for invisibility of the stitching. To place the ears accurately, it may help to turn under the raw edges by ¼in, and sew them together.

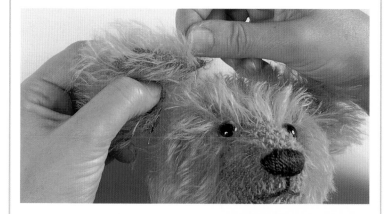

YOU WILL NEED
For stitching the ears
Pair of ears
Colored-headed pins
Extra strong matching color
   thread
Curved needle
Filled bear head

1 Pin both ears to the head using colored-headed or T-shaped pins. Choose the desired position and curvature now, and make sure they are evenly placed; place pins at each end, and also on the back to hold the curvature. Sewing three holding stitches where the pins are will help to hold the ear in place while stitching. Start stitching on the "more difficult" ear, so that it will be easier to attach the second ear to match.

2 Starting on one corner of the first ear, anchor the thread firmly to the head, hiding any securing stitches under the ear. Take the first stitch on the head, just by the corner of the ear.

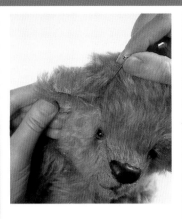

3 | Take the second stitch on the front side of the ear, about ¼in from the raw edge. As usual when using a ladder stitch, take alternate stitches on the two sides to be joined, in this case the ear edge, and the head just below it. Make sure the desired curvature is maintained.

5 | Look at the bear and check that the second ear is still matching the first; adjust the position if necessary. Repeat, using a ladder stitch as for the first ear.

6 | "Jug-handle" ears have to be gathered first. Run a row of ladder stitch along its flat edges.

8 | This type of ear is usually placed more toward the sides of the head, with the corner of the ear just touching the gusset seamline. Stitch in place, using a ladder stitch in the same way as before.

7 | Pull the thread until a slight gathering is achieved. Secure the end so the gathering does not become undone.

4 | When you reach the second corner, turn the bear around and continue using a ladder stitch in the same way around the back of the ear. Go around both sides once more, and take a few back stitches to finish off. If you didn't stitch the raw edges together at the beginning, they will be folded inward as the ear is pulled toward the head.

Finishing Bears

This is the point where bear makers really have the chance to express their creativity. A number of different techniques are described here, but the list is by no means exhaustive. A look through the Gallery pictures will provide some insight on how different artists finish their bears, and suggest inspirational ideas for personalizing your own bear.

A number of techniques can be used to enhance your bear's expression and give it that individual look.

SHAPING THE BEAR You can emphasize the face features by soft-sculpting, which is the process of shaping the bear with a long needle and strong thread. We show how to soft-sculpt the muzzle at eye level, but the same technique can be used to alter the shape of other parts of the bear.

COLORING THE BEAR Real animals have more variegated color in their fur than most fur fabrics, and certain areas might be darker or lighter than the rest. You can try and redress this balance by the judicious application of paint. Airbrushing is another way of doing this, but it is a rather complex technique which is not suitable for explaining here.

FINISHING THE PAWS Real bears have long claws and raised pads on their paws. We will look into ways of representing these in your Teddy Bear.

ANTIQUING One of the charms of antique bears is the fact that they have been deeply loved, and can therefore be rather worn. We will describe the techniques to convert your newly made bear into one that appears old and well loved.

SOFT-SCULPTING

Soft-sculpting is a technique used to create and hold the shape you wish to give your bear. This is done by using a long needle with a length of strong thread and drawing it through the stuffing, so that some areas are indented and others are raised. At each point very small stitches are taken, and each stage is repeated twice to secure the indentation and stop the thread from slipping. The secret is not to pull too strongly on the thread, which may tear the fabric, but to squeeze the bear part and its stuffing so that the path of the thread becomes shorter.

> **YOU WILL NEED**
> **To soft-sculpt**
> Finished bear
> Extra long needle
> Strong thread

2 Taking a tiny stitch, take the needle from under the first eye to under the second eye. Come out at the second eye.

1 Thread the long needle with doubled strong thread. Enter through the back of the head to a point right under the eye. Leave an end of thread hanging at the entry point.

3 Our purpose is to bring the eyes together and make the muzzle a different shape by indenting the sides of its top area. To do this, squeeze the muzzle at the eye point until it has the shape you want. When you put the needle through to go back to the first eye, keep squeezing so that the path of the thread is quite short, pulling the thread gently. Still squeezing, take a small stitch again and go back to the second eye.

4 When the muzzle shape is just as you want it, take the needle and thread to the back of the head on the second side. Finish the ends on both sides by taking small stitches and hiding the ends.

PAINTING

In real bears, certain areas of fur are often a different shade, often darker, and painting the Teddy Bear is a good way to add some realistic color and vary the homogenous look of the fur fabric. The insides of the ears, the area above the eyes, and sections of the muzzle, are places where some touches of paint will enhance the bear's expression.

1 Mix a small amount of acrylic fabric paint, in this case brown, with water in a small container; mix well with a stick. Try the color on a piece of spare fur fabric, mix with other colors, and more or less water, to achieve the desired shade. Using a medium-sized brush, apply the paint to the inside of the ears. Paint in thin layers, and go over as many times as necessary for the fibers to take the color. Remember that paint dries lighter.

2 Touch up the area above the eyes, to give a shaded look that will emphasize the eyes and give them depth. The fur areas will become fairly wet, and they need to be left to dry thoroughly. A hairdryer can be used to speed up the process.

3 Fill your brush with paint again, but this time blot some of the liquid on a wad of paper towel. With this drier brush, lightly touch up the shaved muzzle below the nose and above the mouth.

4 When the paint has dried completely, fluff up the fur areas with a stiff wire brush, to separate the hairs which might have become matted during painting.

EMBROIDERED CLAWS AND PADS

Real bears have claws in their paws and pads, and embroidering is a way to represent this. Colored-headed pins guide the thread that goes over the edge of the paw. The stitches will start on the fur side of the paw, not on the edge where the pins are; these are there to guide the thread to the correct position.

YOU WILL NEED

For embroidering the claws
Finished bear
Embroidery needle, long
Embroidery thread (perle)
   or thin strong (mending)
   wool
Colored-headed pins

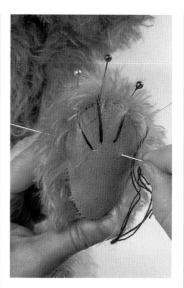

3 When the four stitches are completed, take a tiny back stitch again on the fur side, and then bring the thread out on one side; pull and cut the end off. Repeat on the other paw.

5 Repeat for all four stitches, this time giving them a more pronounced fan shape than for the paws. When finished, come out on one side and secure.

1 Start with the paws. Put four colored-headed pins on the edge of the paw, where the stitches will go. Thread the needle with embroidery thread or thin wool. Take a tiny back stitch on the fur side to secure the end of the thread, and bring the needle out about an inch or so below the first pin, on the suede side of the paw.

2 Loop the thread over the paw, right by the pin, back into the fur side; pull sufficiently so that the thread feels secure. Put the needle back in there, and come out at a point below the second pin. Place the four stitches in a slight fan shape.

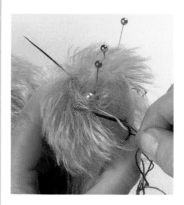

4 Now do the footpads. Secure the end of the thread on the fur side of the foot so it is not visible, loop the thread over the end of the foot by the first pin, and take a stitch as before.

6 Remove the pins and the footpad is ready. Repeat for the second one.

RAISED PAW PADS

Sometimes it is nice to do something a little bit different when making a bear. The paws are one area that can be changed with quite dramatic results. This section shows how to make raised pads out of fine glove leather. Alternatively, other fabrics may be used to create different effects, but the principle remains the same.

YOU WILL NEED
For raised paw pads
Fine glove leather or felt
Sharp scissors
Needle for sewing leather
Extra strong thread
Small amount of soft filling
Forceps
Cut out paws in the same fabric as the bear

1 Cut out the paws in the bear's fabric. Decide how many pads you want and make paper templates. Cut out the fine glove leather a little larger than the template so that the edges can turn under when sewn. Place them onto the paw to determine their position, then trim the fur away from the area that they will cover.

2 Secure the thread to the paw with a few tiny stitches and then using a ladder stitch, start to sew around the pad, turning the edges under as you go.

3 Sew all the way around but leave a small opening. Using fine forceps push a little soft filling, either Kapok or polyester, in between the pad and the paw. Push enough in to raise the pad a little but do not over fill. Continue using a ladder stitch all the way around to the beginning. Push the needle through to the wrong side and then take a few stitches to finish off. Cut the thread but leave a long end.

4 For the paws on the arms, either cut them separately as shown, or cut the underarm and paw piece as one, out of the bear fabric. Sew the pads in place, and then sew this to the outer arm in the normal way.

5 When the foot pads are in place, the paws may be sewn in place in the same way as usual. Do make sure that they are the right way up though. Another method is to sew the pads in place using tiny back stitches instead of a ladder stitch. This picture shows felt pads sewn in this way.

Antiquing or Distressing

The really old bears are wonderful, with their woeful faces and much loved, battered bodies. Unfortunately, even if you can find a nice old bear these days they are often very expensive. The next best thing is to create your own.

Study old bears first and notice what sort of fabrics were used; do not automatically use sparse mohair because in a real old bear the pile is very often worn in patches. Study those patches —the middle of the body for instance or one side of the face. Ears usually wear badly and the eyes may be loose or missing altogether. Maybe there are places where the filling is falling out. Old bears are always grubby, but never really dirty; they have a dusty sort of look and feel, and some of the remaining pile is often matted. They bear scars of many adventures, pencil or crayon marks where injuries have been simulated by over-enthusiastic children at play, and most bears will sport a bald patch where it was treated to the latest in "haute coiffure."

The list of things you will find useful when distressing your bear is just a start. Let your imagination run riot and "see" your bear going through life and build a little history for it; recreate some of the everyday happenings, like a picnic in the garden, a day on the beach, drying out by the fire and getting a little too close. Your bear will have wear and tear—perhaps some holes, or you may prefer to mend them. For some reason old bears were often mended with brightly colored wool in red, blue, or green. You could sew patches in place and mend paws with felt that doesn't match. The list is endless, but remember that you can never make a mistake or ruin it! The worst you can do is to be too neat or too clean. It's hard at first but once you start you will warm to the subject and, by the time it's finished, you will have a bear with a past to be proud of.

ANTIQUING

The bear shown is one that had been made with no intention of distressing it, but it works well to demonstrate some of the techniques that may be used.

YOU WILL NEED
For antiquing
Bear to be antiqued
Scissors
Paints
Forceps
Sandpaper
Paintbrush
Coffee or tea

1 | "Piper" is a 17-in mohair bear, about five years old and much loved.

2 | Use the forceps to pull threads out of the nose. The mouth stitches often come loose or get pulled out altogether. Pluck the pile out of the muzzle; this is one area that would have sustained a lot of friction.

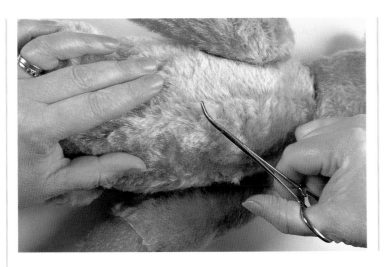

3 | If your bear had a growler, then the area around the middle of the tummy would be worn and have bald patches, or maybe even be split in places where the edges of the growler would have cut the material from the inside.

5 | Mix paints, coffee granules, or strong tea to color and stain patches of your bear. Rub dirt and household dust into the fabric. Mark it with pens or crayons.

6 | Tear part of the pads away and color the wood wool inside so that it is not bright and new.

4 | The top of the arms were also damaged sometimes; the top seam would come undone and the joint disk would show. There would also be some bald patches; chop the pile away roughly using sharp scissors.

Other distressing to this bear that has not been shown includes the following:
● Repeated rubbing against a rough brick wall.
● Sanding of paw pads and glass eyes.
● Loosening of the other glass eye.
● Tearing the ear off.
● Pulling filling out of the body to make it sag.
● Leaving a tight rubber band around the arm to simulate being held and dragged over many years.
● General dirtying of the mohair.
● Holes torn in the suede paw pads.

You should end up with a bear that you would like to clean and mend. You may do this for the ultimate result! If you plan to sell your bear, be sure to label it as a modern bear that has been distressed, to avoid being sued for fraud!

Miniature bears

The nicest things come in
small packages: bears are
no exception.

Miniature Bears

Miniature Bears are a more specialized version of the traditional Teddy Bear. They are currently extremely popular and receiving increased attention from makers and collectors alike. Their size is always less than five inches; three inches and below are even more highly appreciated.

Miniature bears are defined by their scale—they are not small bears, but bears made on a $\frac{1}{12}$th scale, or "an inch to a foot" like all miniatures. The proportions of the bears are the same as for large bears, except that they are done in a smaller scale.

Working in miniature requires different techniques, or variations of ones in use, to produce a bear that is neatly done, accurate, and that achieves the desired effect. As well as knowledge of technique, working in miniature requires good lighting, good eyesight, and nimble fingers. Bright light bulbs, magnifying glasses, and specialized tools are a great help; although they are not substitutes for enthusiasm, accuracy, dedication, and practice.

MATERIALS Short pile mohair fabrics, both sparse and dense, are suitable for miniature bears, but they are more difficult to work with. Upholstery fabrics and cashmere, with a dense pile, are much easier to use, and still have a fur-like appearance. Paws and pads are made in fine Ultrasuede.

Miniature bears are usually stitched by hand. The best thread to use is a clear invisible thread, known as nylon monofilament. Otherwise use cotton or polyester thread in a matching color.

☞
**Suitable types of fabrics, page 14
Specialized tools, page 12
Needles and threads, page 10
Cutting fabrics, page 32
Stitches, page 19**

CUTTING AND STITCHING

A miniature bear pattern is marked and cut in the same way as a big bear pattern, paying attention to the direction of the pile. Seam allowances are $\frac{1}{16}$in and they are not usually marked on the pattern. Trace the pieces very accurately with a non-smudging fine-tip pen, and cut just inside the marked line with very sharp scissors. Stitch with a small needle and invisible or matching-colored thread. Use a running stitch, or a very small back stitch.

YOU WILL NEED

For stitching a miniature bear
Upholstery fabric with a dense pile
Fine Ultrasuede for paws and pads
Sharp scissors
Non-smudging fine-tip pen
Small fine needle (Sharps, or Betweens/Quilting, sizes 12, 11, or 10)
Thread in matching color, or clear invisible thread (nylon monofilament)
Thimble

1 Mark the bear pattern on the back of the fabric, reversing "mirror image" the pieces that require it. Notice that some ear patterns come with the two sides in one piece. Make sure the arrows in the pattern go in the same direction as the pile of the fabric. Mark and cut out all the pieces very precisely, placing them in "bear shape" to help check that all pieces are there.

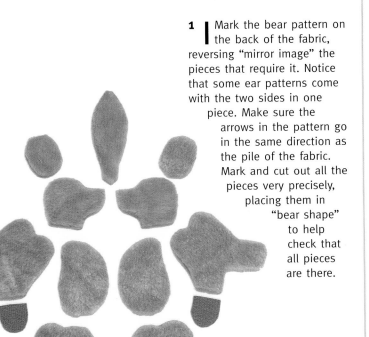

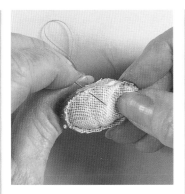

2 Match the two body pieces, right sides together, and starting at one end of the opening, stitch around up to the other end of the opening. Use a very small running stitch; when you reach the other end, come back using the same stitch, but this time filling the gaps left on the way up. Secure the ends very firmly.

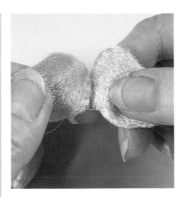

4 Check your stitch tension: if it is too loose, the stitches will be visible on the right side; if it is too tight, the fabric may pucker. Careful stitching now will ensure a better finish later.

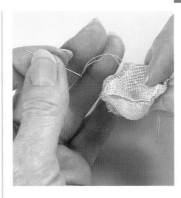

6 Fit the head gusset to the side heads. Start stitching at the center of the nose, and stitch one side first, finishing at the neck. Stitch the second side, from the neck back to the nose.

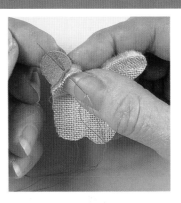

7 With right sides together, attach the paw to the arm using the same stitch.

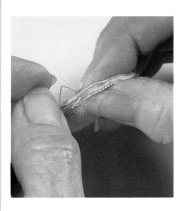

3 As you stitch, pinch the two edges of the fabric together so the backs join, and help the pile stay inside by gently pushing it inward with the needle.

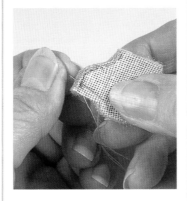

5 Match the two side heads, right sides together, and stitch from the nose down to the neck, using the same stitch as you used for the body.

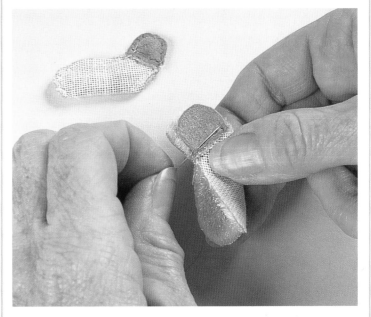

8 Fold the arm over, right sides together, and stitch all around, starting with the paw, and leaving an opening on the side for turning.

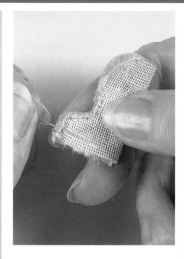

9 Fold the leg in half, right sides together, and stitch the top of the foot area, and a third of the way up the leg.

10 Now fit and stitch the footpad in the same way as explained for the big bear. Use running stitch, as before. Then finish stitching the top of the leg, leaving an opening for turning and stuffing.

11 Fold the ears in half, right sides together, and stitch all around the curved side.

12 With a pair of small sharp scissors, carefully cut a slit on the folded line to make an opening.

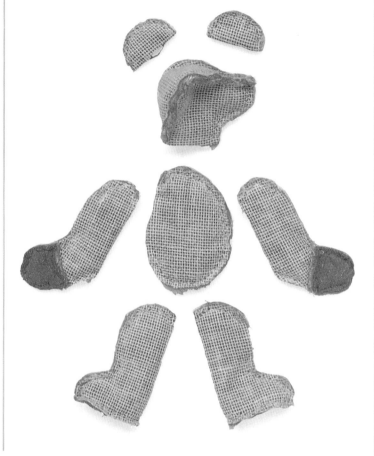

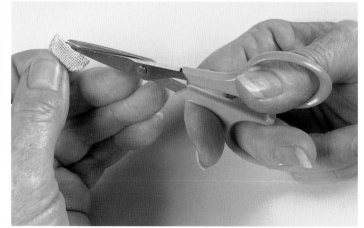

13 The bear is now ready for turning. Check that you have all the pieces and that they fit together correctly.

TURNING

One of the trickiest stages of miniature bear making is the turning process. Take your time and do not rush it; patience and care will bring their rewards. The right tools are a must here: a pair of long tweezers and a pair of narrow forceps or hemostats.

YOU WILL NEED

For turning the bear
Bear pieces to be turned
Pair of long tweezers
Forceps or hemostats

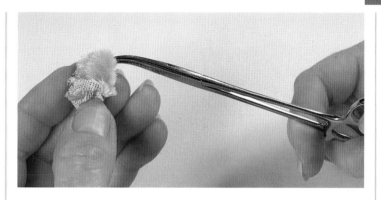

2 Pull the forceps out very gently, while rolling the fabric in the other direction, pushing it right side out.

5 Once turned, use the same tool to push out the seams from the inside.

6 The bear is now turned right side out, and ready for the next stage.

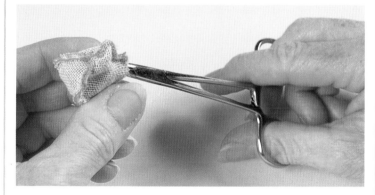

1 The wider pieces, such as the head and the body, should be easily turned with the forceps. Put the tool right into the piece to be turned, grab the fabric at the other end, and lock its jaws.

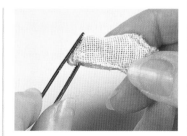

3 The narrower pieces, such as legs, arms, and ears, are best turned with tweezers.

4 Starting at the shoulder end of the arm, insert one prong of the tweezers inside the shoulder, the other prong outside, clamp the tweezers tight, and turn right side out (your tweezer prong that was on the inside should now be on the outside). Now do the other arm. The same technique is applied to the other limbs.

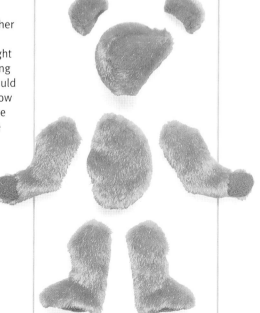

MAKING THE HEAD, AND PLACING THE FEATURES

First the bear head is stuffed, then a miniature cotter pin joint is placed in the neck, and then the features are done. The nose is embroidered, the eyes fitted, and the ears stitched in place, before proceeding to join it to the body.

YOU WILL NEED

For making the head

Miniature unstuffed
    bear head
Polyester stuffing
Miniature cotter pin joint
Small piece of black or
    brown Ultrasuede
Black or brown strands of
    embroidery thread
Colored-headed pins
Two tiny beads for eyes
    (onyx are best, as they
    are perfectly round)
Strong thin thread
Embroidery/crewel needle,
    size 3/4 (for attaching
    the eyes)
Beading needle, size 10/13
    (for embroidering the
    nose)
Small sharp scissors
"Basting" glue

☞

**Fitting a gusset to the
head, pages 36–7
Embroidering a bear's
nose, pages 74–5
Embroidering a bear's
mouth, page 78
Fitting ears, pages 80–1**

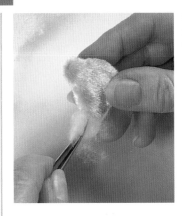

1 | The head has to be stuffed first, using polyester stuffing. Stuff the nose really firmly, and the whole head really well.

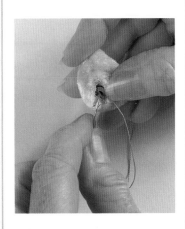

2 | Using strong thread, sew a row of gathering stitches about ⅛in from the fur edge. Place one half of the cotter pin joint (split pin and one disk) inside the head, pull the thread ends and tie tightly. Stitch the ends into the fabric.

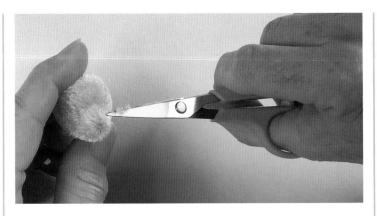

3 | Trim the pile over the nose with sharp scissors.

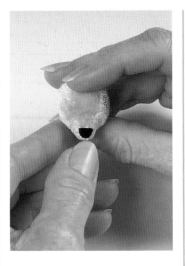

4 | Cut a piece of Ultrasuede in the desired shape of the nose; a sort of inverted triangle with a rounded lower point is good. Attach to the nose area of the head with a dab of glue.

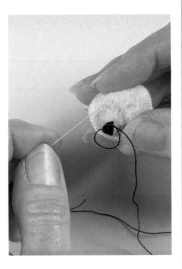

5 | Thread a long needle with one single strand of black or brown embroidery thread. Starting from the neck as close as possible to the joint, come up to the center, just above the nose. Embroider the nose in the same way as for a big bear's nose. Make the mouth in the same way as for a big bear.

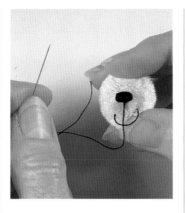

6 When completed, bring the needle out through the neck and finish with several securing stitches.

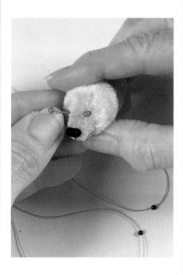

7 Mark the position of the eyes with colored-headed pins (shown here in red). Thread a piece of strong thin thread through each tiny bead.

8 Thread one end through a small embroidery needle (be careful you do not allow the bead to slip off). Put the needle through the head, starting at one eye point, and coming out at the neck. Leave the thread hanging at the base of the neck. Thread the other end on the needle and place the needle beside the first eye point, making a very tiny stitch coming out at the neck beside the first end. Repeat for the other eye.

9 Gently ease down (pull tight) to indent the eye placement, by using your thumb to indent the eye while gently pulling the two threads tight at the neck base. Too much pressure on the threads will break the eye. Knot tightly in place and hide the thread ends in the neck.

11 Stitch them in place with a long needle and matching thread, using a ladder stitch, just like in a large bear.

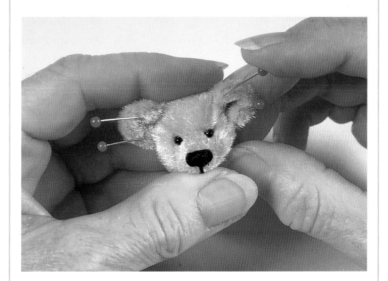

10 Pin the ears evenly to the head; make sure you achieve a pleasing curvature.

STUFFING AND PUTTING JOINTS IN

The head has already been filled, and now the limbs have to be stuffed. First attach the head to the body with the cotter pin joint, then stuff the body, and thread-joint the arms. Other options are to use cotter pin joints in the limbs as well, and to fill the body and limbs with steel shot instead of polyester stuffing.

YOU WILL NEED

To joint and stuff the bear
Polyester stuffing
Embroidery or crewel
    needle
Strong thread
The other half of the
    cotter pin joint
Small awl or other means
    of making tiny holes in
    the fabric
Pair of jeweler's round-
    nose pliers
Colored-headed pins

☞
**Ladder stitch, see
Dictionary of Stitches,
page 19**

1 The bear is now ready to have the joints put in. All the pieces should be turned right side out and the half-cotter pin joint should be protruding from the finished bear's head.

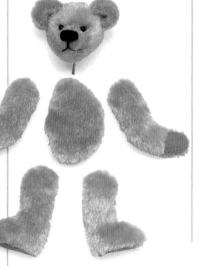

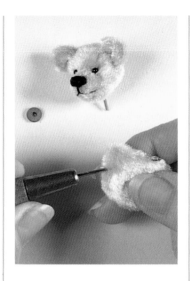

2 Now stuff the arms and the legs firmly with polyester stuffing.

3 Close the openings in the arms and legs using a ladder stitch.

4 Make a hole with the awl on the top of the body, and slip the cotter pin end from the head into it.

5 Place the second disk onto the cotter pin inside the body, and, with the round-nose pliers or cotter key, turn the ends until they form a curl and are sitting firmly on the disk. (Here the technique is shown done in a spare piece of fabric.)

6 | Stuff the body with polyester filling, and close the back using a ladder stitch.

7 | Pin the arms to the body with colored-headed pins, in a position that looks right on the bear, leaving enough "shoulder" space. Look at the bear from all angles, and move the arms up and down to make sure that they are absolutely in line and even.

8 | Using an embroidery or crewel needle and very strong thread, start putting in the joints on one side of the body. Drive the needle across and through one arm, leaving a long end. Take a small stitch and go back through the arm and the body.

9 | Go through the other arm, and back across to the body side of the arm. Tie the two ends very firmly, and hide the ends inside the body and arm.

10 | Pin the legs onto the body with colored-headed pins. Check that the legs are level with the body in the sitting position.

11 | Put joints in the legs with needle and thread in the same way as for the arms.

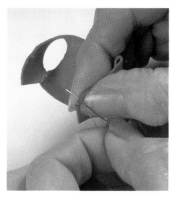

12 | You can make a vest for the bear using Ultrasuede, which is a non-fraying material. Tie a bow around his neck using narrow silk ribbon.

Making garments

What every
self-respecting
bear would
like to wear
about town
and country.

Making Clothes for Bears

Some bears flatly refuse to wear any clothes at all, but if your bear feels he needs more than the suit of fur he was born with there is no need to restrict him to the traditional bow of red ribbon.

Teddy Bear tailoring needs no special skills, but there are a few points to remember. Your choice of fabrics and accessories should take into account the small scale on which you are working. Lightweight, non-fraying fabrics, tiny buttons and snaps, small checks, narrow stripes, and tiny prints are all important to the final result.

Remember a Teddy's rather eccentric proportions when making his clothes—he has long arms, a large head, a fat tummy, maybe a humped back, and legs at the side of his body rather than below it. His clothes must be plenty big enough: pants in particular must be cut very wide, and tops should finish above his legs. Putting a bear's clothes on is much easier if dresses, skirts, and sweatshirts are left open all the way down the back.

PATTERNS AND CUTTING The pattern diagrams reproduced here are approximately half the size required for an average 12in bear, and can be enlarged on a photocopier. (For this size, the bottom straight edge of piece K should measure 6¾in when enlarged.)

If you want to dress another size bear you will need to enlarge the patterns to either more or less than twice the size given here. When using the pattern diagrams follow the line indicated on the key for the garment you are making.

Cut practice patterns out of something flexible like kitchen paper towels or plastic bags, so that you can try the pieces against your bear before cutting into your fabric.

When cutting a left and right piece, remember to reverse the pattern for the second piece, or cut both pieces together from folded fabric.

SEWING METHODS Seam allowances of ¼in are included in the patterns. Seams are sewn by machine, or back stitched by hand, fastening off both ends securely.

Seams are neatened by machine zigzag, or hand over-sewing. Press all seams open unless otherwise stated.

Useful "short cuts" appear in the instructions that follow—using snaps or Velcro instead of buttonholes, and sewing side and underarm seams after finishing the cuff and setting in the sleeve—you are sure to find others.

> **For a 12in bear, enlarge patterns with a photocopier by 200%**

KEY

〰〰〰〰〰〰
Fold

⌒⌒⌒⌒⌒⌒
Knickers cutting line

—·—·—·—·—·—·—·—
Dungarees cutting line

— — — — —
Dress cutting line

·····················
Shirt facing line

– – – – – –
Shirt cutting line

–·–·–·–·–·–
Sweatshirt cutting line

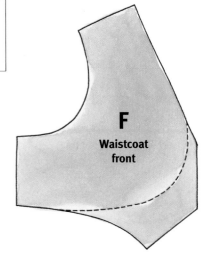

F Waistcoat front

G Waistcoat back

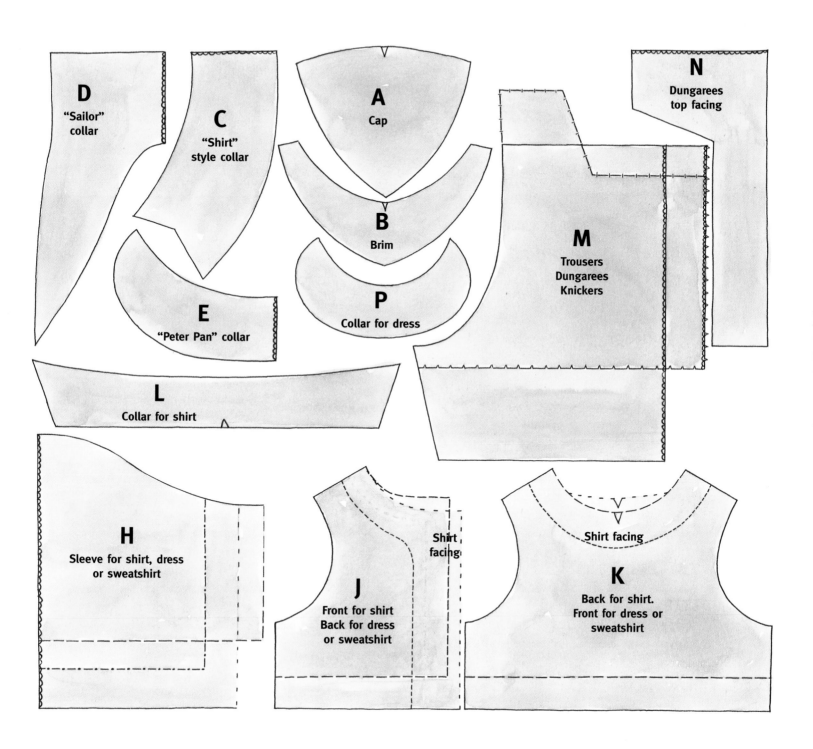

D "Sailor" collar

C "Shirt" style collar

A Cap

B Brim

P Collar for dress

E "Peter Pan" collar

N Dungarees top facing

M Trousers Dungarees Knickers

L Collar for shirt

H Sleeve for shirt, dress or sweatshirt

J Front for shirt Back for dress or sweatshirt

Shirt facing

K Back for shirt. Front for dress or sweatshirt

Shirt facing

Vest and Bow Tie

A vest, perhaps teamed with a matching bow tie, is a basic item in the wardrobe of any well dressed bear.

VEST

Made from a velvet or brocade fabric, this everyday vest can look quite splendid. Use the alternative curved cutting line from the front pattern piece for a different look.

YOU WILL NEED
Lightweight wool or similar fabric
Lining fabric or printed cotton
Two buttons and snaps (optional)

CUTTING
Cut two fronts F (remember to reverse pattern to make a pair, or cut from folded fabric) and one back G, cut on the fold, both in fabric and lining.

1 Press ¼in to the inside on both side edges of the vest and lining back pieces. With right sides together, pin the shoulder seams of the lining. Sew the seam about ¼in from the edges, and do a few back stitches at each end to prevent fraying. Repeat with vest. Press open the seams.

2 With right sides together, pin the lining to the vest all around, matching shoulder seams and all edges. Be sure to keep the side edges of the back turned back on themselves as described in step 1. Stitch all around, leaving both side edges open, and an opening in the back lower edge for turning.

3 With sharp pointed scissors, trim the seam allowance to ⅛in. To give a neat edge when the garment is turned to the right side, clip the curves and corners as shown. Cut the corners diagonally, making sure you do not cut the stitching, and make tiny cuts at right angles to the fabric edge around all curved edges. Be careful not to cut too close!

Turn the vest to the right side, pushing the corners out carefully. Press.

4 To join the side seams, push the raw edges of the front side edges between the pressed edges of the back vest and lining. Slipstitch in place. Then slipstitch the lower back opening.

5 The vest can be fastened with buttons and button holes, or with snaps.

BOW TIE

A small tie like the one shown here is best worn with a vest, or maybe with a plain white cotton collar, but make a larger bow tie and your bear needs nothing more.

YOU WILL NEED

Lightweight cotton or satin
Narrow ribbon (optional)

CUTTING

For the tiny bow here, cut a piece 4in square and a 1in strip long enough to tie around your bear's neck with 2in to spare.

1 Fold the main piece in half with right sides together, stitch the seam, and turn to the right side. Press flat with the seam in the center as shown and oversew the raw edge at each end.

2 Fold the short ends to the center and slipstitch them together.

3 With doubled thread gather the center of the tie as shown. Fasten securely.

4 For the neckband use a piece of matching ribbon. Alternatively, fold a narrow strip lengthwise, stitch along the long edge and turn to the right side with the aid of a darning needle, or, as here, a rouleau turner.

5 Tie the neckband around the finished bow and secure with hand stitching at the back. Tie around your bear's neck.

Collars and Ties

A bear, unlike a human being, can wear a collar and tie on its own, and look smartly dressed and ready for a day at the office!

COLLAR

A plain shirt style collar is illustrated here, but patterns for a sailor collar and a round "Peter Pan" style collar are also given. All of them are made in exactly the same way.

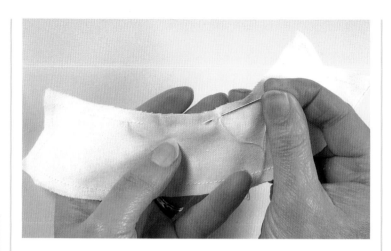

YOU WILL NEED

Fine white cotton or similar fabric
Button or snaps
Trimming (optional)

2 Stitch around the collar, remembering to leave an opening in the shorter curved edge for turning.

3 Trim the seam, and clip the curves and corners, as described for the vest.

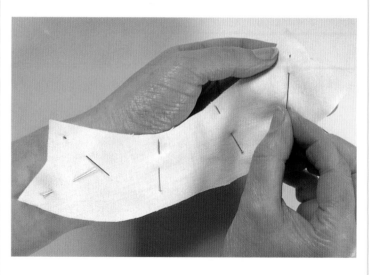

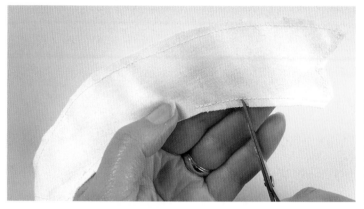

CUTTING

Cut two pieces on the fold (C, D, or E).
Note: The photographs show the shirt style collar C, but all are made in the same way.

1 With right sides together, first pin the collar sections together.

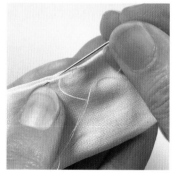

4 Turn to the right side, pushing the corners out with a crochet hook or similar tool. Press well. Slipstitch the opening edges together. Fasten the front with button and buttonhole or snaps.

TIES

This is a standard design which can be varied to suit your bear. The pattern can be cut wider, or you can even make a cravat using the same method.

YOU WILL NEED

Lightweight cotton or satin
Lining fabric (can be the same as main fabric)

CUTTING

Cut a strip of fabric, 12in long: the width at one end should be 4in and at the other 2.5in.
Cut each end to a point, using a full size tie as a pattern.
Cut the identical shape in the lining.

2 Trim the seam, clip the corners, Turn to the right side: a chopstick or crochet hook is useful for pushing out the points and corners.

3 Press the tie well and slipstitch the opening.

1 With right sides together, pin lining to tie. Stitch, leaving an opening for turning.

4 Place tie flat with lining upward, and fold both long sides to meet in the center. Press well and then slipstitch the edges together.

Hats

Sometimes a hat is all the clothing a bear needs, as this schoolboy bear demonstrates. The peaked cap, as shown here however, adds the finishing touch to the bear's outfit.

SCHOOL CAP & SCARF
The scarf is a strip of fabric cut to size and fringed at the ends. If the fabric frays easily, overcast the long edges.

YOU WILL NEED
Double sided blanket fabric, felt or other firm fabric
Stretch ribbing

CUTTING
Cut four cap pieces (A) and two brim pieces (B).

1 For each half, pin and stitch two cap pieces together. Place both halves together matching the seams, and join the center seam. Turn to the right side and press.

2 With right sides together pin and stitch two brim pieces together. Trim the seam, turn, and press. Stitch close to the pressed edge.

3 Pin the brim to the cap, matching the center of the brim to the center of one crown section and making sure that the raw edges are even. Stitch, fastening off the ends securely.

4 Cut a band from stretch ribbing. This should be twice the desired width of the band and long enough to fit around the cap when slightly stretched. Join the short ends of the band, fold it in half lengthwise, right sides out, and pin to the lower edge of the cap, enclosing the brim. Stitch the band to the cap and finish the seam with a machine zigzag stitch or oversew by hand.

5 Turn the front of the band to the inside under the brim as shown.

PEAKED CAP

Make a cap to match a boy bear's dungarees, or one to match a girl bear's skirt.

YOU WILL NEED
Firm cotton or similar

CUTTING
To make the pattern draw a circle with a radius of 1¼ in for the hat top, and a strip 1¼in by 9in for the hat side.
Cut two hat tops, one hat side, and two brims (B).

2 | Pin the brim to the center of one side piece, right sides together. Tack the brim in place. With right sides together, place the other side piece (the facing) over the first and pin around the lower edge of the cap. Stitch the seam through all the thicknesses, enclosing the brim.

3 | Turn the facing to the inside, press well, and tack the raw edges together. Place the top of the cap in position as shown.

4 | Pin the cap top to the sides. Stitch and overcast the seam. Finally turn the cap to the right side.

1 | Pin and stitch the short ends of both side pieces, making two circles. Press the seams open. With right sides together, pin the two brim pieces together. Stitch around the long curved edge. Trim the seam, clip the curves, turn to the right side, and press well. Stitch the raw edges of the brim together.

Skirt

This bear wears a simple skirt and vest with a white cotton "Peter Pan" collar. Peeping from under her skirt is a pair of lace-trimmed bloomers.

SKIRT AND VEST

The skirt is made from two pieces of fabric. The vest is cut from Ultrasuede and needs no lining or binding. The vest and collar were embroidered by machine.

YOU WILL NEED
Plain or patterned cotton
or cotton mix fabric
Snaps

CUTTING
Cut one waistband 11in by 1¼in and one skirt piece 5in by at least 24in.

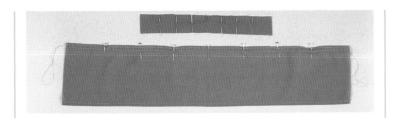

1 Press ¼in to the inside along the lower edge of the skirt, then turn up another ¼in and stitch close to the pressed edge.

2 Sew a double row of gathering stitches along the top edge of the skirt.

3 With pins, mark half, quarter, and eighth points on the upper edge of the skirt and the lower edge of the waistband.

4 With right sides together, pin skirt to waistband, matching marker pins. Put in extra pins, distributing the fullness of the skirt evenly along the waistband.

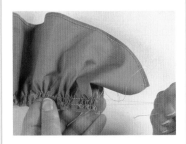

5 Gently pull up the gathering threads, being careful not to pull so hard that you break the threads. Distribute the gathers evenly and make sure that the waistband is lying flat.

6 Stitch the skirt to the waistband. Run the machine slowly so that you can leave the pins in until you have sewn right up to each one. In this way, the gathers will remain evenly placed. Stitch again, within the seam allowance, and close to the first line of stitching to strengthen the seam. Trim seam and remove the gathering threads. Press seam up toward the band.

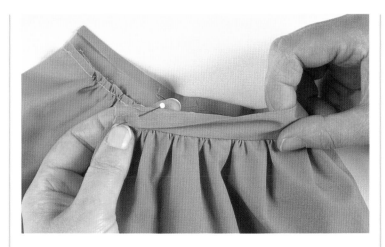

10 Slipstitch the pressed edge of the waistband to the seam. Try the skirt on the bear and fasten the waistband with snaps.

7 Press ¼in to the inside along the top edge of the waistband. Fold the waistband to the outside, placing the pressed edge level with the waist seam.

8 Stitch across both ends of the waistband. Finish the back edges of the skirt with a machine zigzag stitch as shown.

9 Turn the waistband to the inside. Press ¼in to the inside down both back edges. Stitch close to inner edge, over zigzag stitching.

Dress

Here is a very feminine dress to enchant any little girl bear. The matching bloomers are made according to the pants pattern, but cut wider, with the lower edge of each leg trimmed with lace and elastic as described for the dress sleeves.

YOU WILL NEED

Cotton or cotton mix fabric—we used a tiny flower print
Fine white cotton for the collar and lining
Cord elastic
Snaps

☞
Trimming seams in Vest section, page 102
Gathering in Skirt section, pages 108–109
Dress collar in Collars section, pages 104–105

CUTTING

Cut one front piece K in patterned fabric and lining, two back pieces J (left and right) in patterned fabric and lining, two sleeves H, and one skirt piece 5in by at least 24in, and four collar pieces P in white fabric.

1 Place the two collar sections right sides together, pin and stitch, leaving the whole neck edge (the shorter curved edge) open. Trim the seam, turn, and press. Make two collar sections and slipstitch them together at the front corners, keeping your stitches inside the $\frac{1}{4}$in seam allowance.

2 Pin fronts to back at shoulder seams. Repeat for lining. Stitch seams, securing seam ends with back stitching. Press seams open.

3 Pin the collar to the right side of the dress, matching the point where the two collar sections meet with the center of the dress front. Pin all around (the ends of the collar will not quite reach the back edges of the dress). Now match the completed lining to the dress and pin the back and neck edges, right sides together, matching seams and corners, and sandwiching the collar between the dress and the lining.

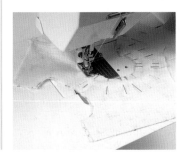

4 Stitch the lining to the dress at the back and neck edges as pinned, making sure the collar is secured. Trim seam, clip curves, and cut corners diagonally as described for the vest.

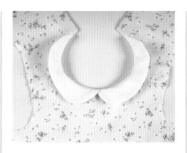

5 Turn the lining to the inside and press carefully. Stitch the lining to the dress at the armhole edge, keeping your stitching inside the seam allowance.

6 Trim the lower edge of the sleeve with lace. With the right side facing up, place the edge of the lace level with the raw edge of the sleeve. Stitch in place. Finish the edge with machine zigzag or hand oversewing.

7 Turn the lace downward and press the seam up. With the right side up, stitch along the pressed edge. Cut two pieces of cord elastic to fit the bear's upper arm plus 1in. Tie a knot near each end. Using a medium width zigzag, machine stitch the elastic to the wrong side of the sleeve about 1in from the lower edge, stretching the elastic as you stitch by holding it at each end as shown. Stitch several times over the knots to secure the elastic at each end.

8 Stitch two rows of gathering threads around the top of the sleeves. Pin the sleeves into the armholes, distributing the gathers evenly. Pull up the gathering threads and stitch the seam. Trim the seam and finish it with a zigzag stitch.

9 Fold the sleeve in half lengthwise, with right sides together, and pin the underarm seam, matching the armhole seam and edges. Stitch the seam, trim, and finish with zigzag stitch.

10 Sew a double row of gathering threads along the top edge of the skirt. Make a narrow hem along the bottom edge and both back edges. Join the bodice to the skirt in the same way as the waistband is joined to the skirt on pages 108–109. Try the dress on the bear and sew snaps at the neck and waist.

Pants

This versatile pattern can be used in many ways: cut wider to make underpants, or shorter to make shorts. The t-shirt is made from knitted cotton fabric. Cut the t-shirt and lining using the dress bodice pattern, omitting the collar. Follow the instructions for the lined vest on page 102.

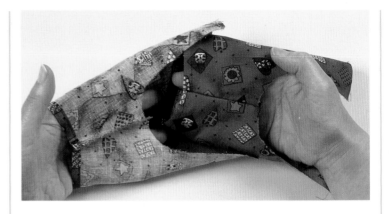

CUTTING	YOU WILL NEED
Cut two pieces (M) on folded fabric.	Light to medium weight cotton, needlecord, lightweight wool, etc. Elastic, ¼in wide

1 Hem the lower edge of each pant leg. Turn ¼in to the inside and press. Turn the pressed edge to the inside and stitch in place. Fold each leg in half lengthwise with right sides together and stitch straight inner leg seam. Finish off seam. Press seams open.

2 Turn *one* leg right side out, and place this leg inside the other with inner leg seams matching, right sides together. Pin and stitch the crotch seam from center front to center back.

3 Stitch the crotch seam again around the curved upper thigh part. Trim the seam, clip the curves, turn, and press well.

4 To form the waistband, turn ¼in to the inside around the top of the pants and press. Turn pressed edge to the inside, forming a waistband ½in deep. Press again. Stitch close to the top pressed edge, and again close to lower pressed edge leaving a small opening to insert the elastic. Using a bodkin, thread the elastic through the waistband. Try the pants on your bear, pull up the elastic to fit, and tie the ends together firmly.

Tracksuit

This casual tracksuit gives your bear a delightful sporty look. It is cut using a variation of the pants pattern and the dress bodice pattern.

CUTTING

Cut two trouser pieces, M, cut on the fold, one front K, two backs J (left and right), two sleeves H. Remember to use the tracksuit cutting lines. Cut a strip of ribbing 2.5in wide.

YOU WILL NEED

Fleece-backed cotton
Stretch ribbing
Elastic

3 For the sweatshirt, join the shoulder seams. Cut the ribbing to fit the bear's lower arms and neck, and apply it to the sleeves and neck edges as above. Set in the sleeves and join the side seams as given for the dress (see pages 110–111). Finish off the raw edges along the back and lower edges with a machine zigzag stitch, press ¼in to the inside, and stitch in place.

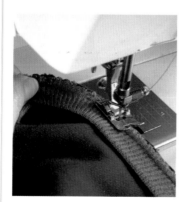

1 Cut two pieces of ribbing to fit the bear's ankle. Fold the band in half lengthwise and pin the raw edges to the bottom of the pant leg right sides together, stretching the band to fit. Stitch, using the narrowest possible zigzag stitch.

2 Finish off the seam, using a wider zigzag to enclose the raw edges. Continue exactly as for the pants on page 112.

Dungarees

These dungarees with their matching cap look good worn over a tartan shirt, but many bears just wear them over their fur!

CUTTING
Cut two of piece M on the fold. Remember to use the cutting line for the dungarees, which includes the front bib piece at the top, and the longer length. Cut off the bib at the back. Cut the facing N on the fold and two straps, 7in by 2in.

YOU WILL NEED
Medium weight cotton fabric
¼in elastic
Two buttons
Snaps or Velcro (optional)

3 Pin the raw edges of the straps to the back of the dungarees about 1in on either side of the back seam, and angled as shown.

2 Turn the straps to the right side, using a crochet hook or something similar to push the corners completely out. Press well. Continue in the same way as for pants, steps 1–3, shown on page 112.

5 Pin the facing to the top of the dungarees with right sides together and matching seams and corners. Stitch around the top edge of the facing, stitching through all thicknesses, enclosing the open ends of the straps.

1 Fold each strap piece in half lengthwise with right sides together, and stitch across one end and along the long edge. Trim the seam and cut the corners diagonally.

4 With right sides together pin and stitch the short straight edge at the back of the dungarees' facing. Press the seam open. Overcast the lower edge of the facing either by hand or with a machine zigzag stitch.

6 | Trim the seam. Snip the seam allowance to the stitching at the inner corners as shown, and trim the outer corners diagonally.

7 | Turn the facing to the inside, making sure the corners are as square as possible. Press well. On the outside, stitch around the top close to the pressed edge. To form the casing for the elastic, stitch around the back waist again about ¹/₂in from the first stitching, starting and ending the stitching level with the sides of the bib as shown.

8 | Using a bodkin, thread the elastic through the casing. Use a piece of elastic that is long enough to prevent its being pulled completely through the casing.

9 | Stitch across the casing, through the elastic, placing your stitches in line with the top-stitching along the sides of the bib, drawing the elastic up to fit your bear. Trim the ends of the elastic, not too close to the stitching.

10 | Try the dungarees on your bear and fasten the straps to the bib with buttons and button holes, or, to make it easier, do as we have done here and use small pieces of Velcro stitched to the strap ends and the inside of the bib. You can sew decorative buttons on the outside.

Shirt

A classic front buttoned shirt with collar and cuffs is another essential item. The shorts worn with this shirt are made to the pants pattern, cut to length, using sweatshirt fabric.

YOU WILL NEED

Cotton or cotton mix fabrics
Four small buttons
Four snaps (optional)
Iron-on interfacing

CUTTING

Cut one back K, two fronts J (left and right), two sleeves H, two collars L, and two cuffs 1½in by 1½in. Cut two front facings left and right and a back neck facing using the upper part of pieces J and K as marked by the dotted line.

1 Place two collar sections right sides together, pin and stitch, leaving the whole neck edge (the shorter curved edge) open. Trim the seam, turn, and press.

☞
Shirt collar in Collars section, pages 104–105

2 Pin the fronts to the back at the shoulder seams. Stitch by hand or machine, making a ¼in seam. Press the seam open.

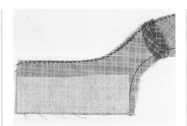

3 Stitch the front facings to the back facing at the shoulder seams. Press the seams open. Apply a strip of iron-on interfacing to the straight inner edge of the front facing as shown. Overcast the long curved outer edge of the entire facing. Machine stitch around the neck edge, inside the seam allowance, on the shirt and facing, and make tiny cuts, up to the stitching, as described for the vest on page 102.

4 Pin the open edge of the collar to the right side of the shirt neck edge, matching center points, and having raw edges even. The collar will *not* reach the front edge of the shirt. Stitch, making a seam of less than ¼in.

5 Pin the facing to the shirt over the collar, with right sides together and matching shoulder seams and edges. Stitch the facing to the shirt all around the unfinished edge starting at the bottom, going up the front, around the neck edge, down the other front, and across the bottom of the facing. Trim the corners and clip the curves as shown.

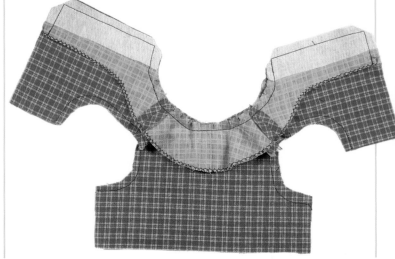

   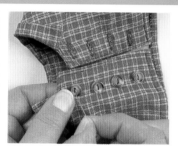

6 Turn the facing to the inside and press well. On the outside, stitch close to the finished front edges and around the neck below the collar. Work a row of stitches less than ¼in from the armhole edges to strengthen. Clip the edge to the stitching as shown.

8 Fold sleeves in half lengthwise, matching cuff and underarm seams. Pin and stitch the entire sleeve and side seams, from the lower edge of the shirt to the lower edge of the cuff.

9 On the cuff edge, turn ¼in to the inside and press. Fold the cuff in half and slipstitch the pressed edge to the seam. Repeat with the other sleeve. Press the lower edge of the shirt to the inside, level with the lower edge of the front facing. Slipstitch this in place, tucking the raw edge under as you stitch.

10 Make button holes in the left front band and sew on buttons to correspond. Alternatively, sew on snaps under the buttons.

7 Pin the cuffs to the lower edge of the sleeves, matching the edges and centers, and pleating the sleeves to fit. Stitch the seams and press them toward the cuffs. Pin the sleeves into the armholes, matching centers and edges, pleating to fit. Stitch the seams, trim and overcast raw edges.

An inspirational showcase
of the work of some of our
leading bear artists to whet
your appetite and fire your
imagination.

Gallery

Bear Inspirations

The collection of bears we present here should prove inspirational for bear makers as well as collectors. From the traditional early bears to the amazing creations of some of the contemporary bear artists, we are dazzled by the way the Teddy Bear has continued to evolve. You can admire the craftsmanship and artistry of these bear makers, or use their examples as a stepping stone to design and make your own creations.

TRADITIONAL BEARS

Old traditional bears are so very appealing that we would all like to have one. Unfortunately, they are not only expensive, but also hard to come by. The choice is to buy an actual replica of an old bear, made either by a bear artist or by a traditional bear manufacturer, such as Steiff, Merrythought, or Dean. Or, we can buy a modern bear that has been designed and made to look very much like the old fashioned ones, and in some cases has been "antiqued" to look old. The real challenge of course, is to make your own bear.

◄ LIONEL
Iris and Ches Chesney of H. M. Bears

Lionel is a replica of a 1907 American bear, 16in tall. He is made from Yorkshire mohair, with glass eyes, wood wool filling, and is fitted with a growler. He has been made to look like a much loved bear, showing all the wear and tear of an old family friend. Through the use of clippers, files, pliers, and crayons, plus the use of wood wool filling, the bear has the look and feel of one who has reached a great age.

▲ JOSEPH
Keith Freeman and Susan Tailby of Bear Paws Collectables

This 12½in bear was made with an old piece of mohair and genuine antique shoe button eyes. Stuffed with antique old straw filling, he has wool felt pads, lined with iron-on cotton so they are more hard-wearing. His nose has been layered with beeswax after embroidery, and he wears a pale blue ribbon with a wire edge.

◀ BASIL
Steiff
This very early bear, circa 1920, is 25in high. Made in pale golden/honey mohair, fully jointed, with two-toned colored eyes (brown with a black pupil), its growler still works. He is in excellent condition, and would be the pride of any collection. He also provides the inspiration for bear makers who want to make Teddies that look like early models.

▼ RALPH
Merrythought
Designed by John Axe, Ralph is a modern Merrythought bear, produced in the original factory at Ironbridge in Shropshire, using traditional techniques.

▶ ZOTTY
Steiff
Here is a modern replica made by Steiff of its own early bear with an open mouth. It is made from caramel/white tipped mohair, fully jointed, and displays the Steiff characteristic mark, the "button in ear."

CLASSIC BEARS

Classic bears, made by contemporary bear-makers and artists in a traditional way, are always popular. They have all the characteristics of old bears: long arms, long snouts, and beautifully soft mohair coats. These are the type of bears most makers would like to make first. Here we have a wonderful selection—slim and plump, sad and happy—to inspire us in the search for our own style.

▼ TERRYCOTTER
Helen West of Cloth Ears
This 15in bear is made in sparse mohair in a terracotta shade, with suede paws and pads. He is part-pellet filled to give him his slumped look. He has glass eyes and a hand embroidered nose. He is an original creation, and was nominated for the British Bear Awards.

▼ CLAUS
Mary Holden of Only Natural
Claus is a 14½in chunky bear, made in old gold sparse mohair, with leather paws and pads, and jointed with nut and bolt joints. He is filled with sheep's wool, a natural material which the maker prefers, and which has received an award of excellence for safe fillings.

▲ BARNEY
Rosita Lynn of Old Bexley Bears
This 21in bear is made in green/gold long curl mohair, with black Austrian glass eyes, a hand embroidered waxed nose, and a graduated clipped muzzle with inverted Y-shape mouth. It has long curved arms and long legs, both with Ultrasuede pads, and a traditional body shape with hump and growler.

▼ GULLIVER
**Wendy Mullany of
Atlantic Bears**
One of Wendy Mullany's larger bears, Gulliver is 28in tall, and one of a limited edition of 50. He is made in golden German mohair, with pure wool felt pads, and reproduction shoe button eyes. He is completely stuffed with wood wool and has cotter pin joints.

▲ DAMIAN
Alicia Merrett
Damian is a small, happy-looking 8in bear. one of the artist's new series of "Sit-in-your-Hand" bears. He is made in a feathery sparse mohair, with Ultrasuede pads, black glass eyes, and is filled with a mixture of polyester and pellets.

◄ HERBIE
**Diana Oldacre of
Oldacre Bears**
Herbie is an 18in traditional
style bear with a rather
plaintive expression. It is
made in medium length pile
crushed mohair, with black
glass eyes, and is filled
partially with pellets, which
helps give it its slumped look.

◀ WOODY
Sue Schoen of Bocs Teganau
Woody is a 16in plump bear made in golden brown, thick curly mohair, and stuffed with a mixture of pellets and polyester filling. He has Ultrasuede pads with hand stitched claws and black glass eyes, and his neck has been fitted with a double neck joint that allows flexible head movements. He is one of a group of "Star-Gazing Bears," inspired by the appearance of the Hale-Bopp comet.

▼ CEDRIC
Jill Hussey of Something's Bruin
This is a large, floppy character bear in light colored long fiber mohair, with the shaped, sculpted, and embroidered pads that are characteristic of this artist. He has small, side placed ears, and a shaped and sculpted muzzle. His nose was created in a particularly unusual way: thickly embroidered first in brown thread and then oversewn with light colored embroidery thread in clearly separate stitches.

EVOLUTION OF THE CLASSIC BEAR

Tradition is important, but we cannot stop evolution. Bear artists are creative people and do not want to confine themselves to just one style. So Teddy Bears have been slowly acquiring new shapes, becoming more realistic, or less realistic, departing just slightly from tradition or moving straight into the realm of fantasy. The result is variety, with room for creativity and imagination.

◄ GRANVILLE
Melanie and Paul Newton of F. J. Hannay
A 10in bear made in long, sparse distressed mohair, Granville is unusual in having a tail and eyebrows. The eyebrows give a special expression to the bear, which also has a long snout, a big embroidered nose, and a smiling mouth. His ears are attached low down on the sides of the head. He wears a hand knitted wool tank top and stands by himself very well, balancing his body on his large feet and strong legs.

▼ CYRIL
Barbara Ann Bears
Cyril is a two-tone mohair bear with a double neck joint, bent, narrow knees, eyelids and eyelashes, and a sculpted head. Pellets fill parts of the limbs, especially the knees, and the tummy area, to give weight and balance. The contrasting lengths of mohair really bring out the bear character, especially as different colors are used. The double neck joint and shaped additional neck piece give a lot of freedom of movement and of expression.

BEARS ON ALL FOURS

Before the advent of the Teddy Bear, in 1903, there were many other toy bears; in Europe they were collectively named "Bruin." Many of those bears were made to stand on four legs. A few of those bears slipped into the early collections of the manufacturers, such as Steiff, and they are now being replicated. After a period of absence, the bear "on all fours" is making a comeback as part of the "realistic bear" group of makers. These bears are very attractive, looking somewhere between Teddy Bears and real bears, and they serve to remind us of the real origins of the Teddy Bear.

▼ MONTY
Sue Tolcher of Hembury Bears
This bear was given the name Monty because he is a bare bear, depicted "on the fur." He is a 20in-long bear with a distinctly shaped double neck joint, and a tail. His front legs are longer than the back ones, so he can sit on his hind legs. His fur is made from British mohair with mixed-colored strands of hair. His ears are small, like those of real bears, and his nose has been waxed with several layers, and then polished, so that it also looks more realistic.

▲ BEAR ON WHEELS
Sue and Randall Foskey of The Nostalgic Bear Co., U.S.A.
This bear, photographed here without its wheels, is a reproduction of an antique bear. The 15in-tall and 19in-long bear is fiber filled, and made in antique cinnamon, dark backed, sparse mohair, with wool felt paw pads. It has glass eyes and its head is jointed, but not its limbs.

► MISTY BEAR
**Richard and Lisa Gunston of
Wood-U-Like Bears**
Misty Bear, from the artists'
Life-Like series, is made with
1in German tipped mohair. He
stands on all fours and can
be posed upright. All the
limbs have their own "flexi-
units." The head is hand
sculpted, the eyes realistic
with molded lids. It is a "Yes-
No" bear, fitted with the
maker's unique mechanism,
which produces a head
movement effect similar to
one used in a number of
antique toys.

◄ MOTHER BEAR
AND CUBS
**Gregory Gyllenship of
Gregory Bears**
This is a one-of-a-kind set of
challenging six-jointed bears.
Although portrayed more
realistically, and equally
comfortable on four legs or
two, they are essentially
Teddy Bears.

SPECIAL FEATURES

Another way of making bears look a bit different is by adding special features and finishes: needle sculpting, painting, airbrushing, adding raised or painted paw pads, making open mouths, or shaving the muzzle in a different way.

▲ FLINT
Sue Smith of Soulmate Bears
Flint is a 24½in American black bear. He comes from a collection of American History Bears, which portray real bears as they should be, fishing and hunting in freedom, away from cruelty and captivity. He is made from dark brown alpaca, and his pads are made from a recycled fur coat. Leather is used for the individual pads, for the embroidered claws and for his sculpted nose and mouth. He has small ears, realistic "buzzard" eyes with veins, and a tail, and is holding a carved wooden fish.

▲ MICKEY LEE
Brigette Peacock and Jean Ball of Burlington Bearties
Mickey is a 16in-tall bear made in short, velvety, pale beige mohair. He is one of four of a very small special edition and has hand painted features with the special feature of an open mouth.

▼ GARRISON
Alison Morton of Brodie Bears
Approximately 29in high, Garrison is made in English mohair, fully jointed, and filled with polyester and pellets. Among his special features are a hand painted and needle sculpted face, and glass eyes fitted in leather eye sockets. He also has raised pads on fur fabric footpads. This one-of-a-kind bear was made for a special celebration, some of the proceeds of which were donated to charity.

▼ COCOA
Anita Hill
Cocoa is an 18in, fully jointed bear, He was made from dark brown tipped alpaca, with sparse mohair muzzle and pads in beige. He is polyester and pellet filled, has glass eyes, and lock nut and bolt joints. His face and his pads are delicately airbrushed onto fur fabric. His nose is coated with a special sealer to make it shine.

▶ BORIS
Sue Tolcher of Hembury Bears
Boris, a 26in bear, is made in extra dense alpaca, jointed, and with quite special feet that are quilted and stuffed, and paw pads made from Ultrasuede. Other features of Sue Tolcher's bears include tails and waxed noses.

◀ BERTRAND
Lisa and Richard Gunston of Wood-U-Like Bears
Bertrand is an 11in bear made in a mohair fabric with a hint of pink on a dark woven background. He is very unsusual because his eyes have both pupil and conjunctiva and are fitted from the rear into sockets and lids. He has a unique embroidered nose with nostrils surrounded by the black embroidery thread. A special "Yes-No" mechanism, mostly carved in wood, is fitted in the neck.

SIMPLE CLOTHES

Bears "on the fur" are delightful—but they may also look wonderful when dressed. Many bears only need very simple clothes: a bow or a collar, a knitted sweater, or some antique piece of baby clothing. Let the look of the bear itself determine whether it wants to be dressed or not.

◄ GRETEL
Jan Galleymore of My Old Teddy
Gretel is 15in tall, made in distressed sparse fur, and with Austrian green eyes. She has legs cut in a bent shape so she can actually sit on an edge, but they are hidden by her outfit, an old baby's dress which was inspired by the maker's love for old lace and old style clothes. The golden chain, with a cat at the end, is modern.

▲ DANNY
Annie Davis of Malvern Bears
This one-of-a-kind 12in smiling bear, was made in tipped mohair with wool felt pads. He was made soft and squeezable by a mixture of polyester and pellets for stuffing. The muzzle is hand-clipped with scissors. His cardigan is hand knitted.

▶ TOBIAS
Andrew and Julie Hubbard of Mother Hubbard
Tobias is a lovingly-made 20in bear in cinnamon mohair, with black glass eyes and polyester filling, and is fully jointed. He is wearing a very suitable pair of dungarees.

▼ ALEXANDER
Naomi Laight
This is a gold plush fur fabric bear, filled with Kapok, and very hard packed in the maker's inimical style. The knitted sweater is a trademark of Naomi's earlier bears.

▲ CHRISTIE
Jennie Sharman-Cox of Mister Bear
Christie is a traditional, old fashioned bear, 18in tall, made in English mohair and typically representative of the maker's work. He wears a Fair Isle knitted sleeveless sweater.

UNUSUAL COSTUMES

Costumes can be different without being complex. Many bear artists choose clothing made from antique fabrics, to represent their bears in historical settings or as special characters from history. Others prefer to dress their bears in costumes that give them a modern feel or a particular personality.

▶ WOOL BEAR
Marie Robishin of Germany

This one-of-a-kind bear is made from vintage fabrics. Made from woollen fabric, this bear has a leather nose and black eyes, and is stuffed with a traditional filling, originally called "excelsior" and now known as wood wool. He wears leather dungarees and a jacket with gold buttons, both also made from antique fabrics, and a knitted scarf.

◀ FRAZER
Sue Tolcher of Hembury Bears

Frazer is a 20in character bear, the equivalent of "a gruff looking old man." He is made from shiny, silky mohair, and has contrasting cream colored whiskers and inserts into his ears. His head is stuffed with wood wool and his body is filled partly with pellets and partly with real wool from the mills at Buckfast Abbey in England. He is dressed with a hand knitted sweater, and a hat with a pompom. He sports a charity pin.

► SYBIL
**Gloria Norbury from
Norbeary Bears**
Sybil is a 12in "ragged little
urchin making the best of
life," from the "Raggamuffins"
collection. With their interest
in antiques, the makers try to
achieve a well-worn, ragged,
"found in a charity shop" look
by using different antiquing
techniques to make their
bears look old. They
use traditional
mohair for the
body, suede pads,
and black glass
eyes, although they
have made a
concession to
modern materials for
the stuffing, and use a
mixture of polyester and
pellets which together give
the bear the desired cuddly
and floppy feel.

▼ JAN
Yvonne Plakké of Holland
Jan is 12in tall, made from
medium length beige
distressed mohair, filled with
pellets and polyester, and
with black eyes. He wears an
unusual costume of red and
white checked pants, a straw
hat, and carries a scarecrow.

▼ BRITISH TOMMY
**Jennie Sharman-Cox of
Mister Bear**
British Tommy is a 16in-tall
bear, made of sparse
distressed mohair, with old
shoe button eyes, and part
pellet filled. His First World
War uniform is made from
original fabric, and he sports
old medals.

HOMEY BEARS

Some bears look and feel especially homey. They can be dressed and posed as a family, or they can simply be cuddly, babyish bears that remind you of a child. Mothers and cubs complete the picture.

▼ HOME SWEET HOME
Jo Greeno
This large size display was made for Teddy Bear Kingdom, the new Museum at Huis Ten Bosh, Asia's largest theme park, which opened in late 1997. It is a complete family scene with fully dressed mother, father, and three children sitting around a table with their dog.

▲ CINDERS
Elizabeth Lloyd from Cupboard Bears
Cinders is only 11in tall, made in soft biscuit colored mohair with Ultrasuede paw pads. She is wearing a blue and tan checked dress, patched near the knee, with a matching ribbon in her ear.

◀ CRISPIN
Sonya Heron of Australia from Enchanted Bears
Like all true artists' bears, Crispin is entirely handcrafted by his maker from her original design, and made in hand-dyed German mohair. He is an old fashioned bear dressed in a sailor outfit, shown playing with his handmade boat.

▲ WOLFERL
Renate Hanisch of Austria
Wolferl is made from long wavy mohair and is wearing a simple sailor collar. Renate's bears often have paws made from deer skin, and the filling is a mixture of polyester and pellets in different grain sizes. She uses "flexilimbs" and other special jointing mechanisms to achieve a variety of poses.

◀ RUSSELL
Hilary Clark
Russell is an 18in "Sleepyhead" bear. He is a collectors' bear made especially for children using safety joints and eyes. Made in hand-dyed mohair, he has an embroidered nose and a growler in his polyester-filled tummy. This type of bear is a great favourite as a christening present.

PAIRS OF BEARS

Sometimes two bears together amount to more than the sum of their parts. A pair can comprise a couple, a parent and child, two siblings, or just two friends. They can just simply be together or have clothes or props that add to the meaning. Whatever it is, their friendship and companionship are very appealing. When you are making your own Teddies, think about making a pair of one kind or another—it seems to add to their loveability.

▲ OH WHAT A PANTOMIME
**Paula Lawton from
Paula-Bears**
This is one pair from a "masquerade" collection of bears dressed as various animals. The artist is attempting to introduce some humor and wit to the constant search for individualism in bear making.

◄ BETSY AND BEN
**Linda Edwards of
Little Treasures**
Betsy and Ben are a 7½in-tall pair of bears in golden mohair, with glass eyes, cotter pin joints, and embroidered claws. The artist likes making pairs of bears with coordinated garments, which are very popular.

▼ MUMMY PLEASE MAKE
TEDDY WELL . . . AGAIN!
**Teresa Rowe from Waifs
and Strays**
The artist enjoys making
showpieces, with bears of
distinctive character and
personality. Her trademark is
attention to fine detail and
well-tailored costumes.

▲ BOBBINS
**Sue Quinn of
Dormouse Designs**
Bobbins are a pair of small
bears made in distressed
mohair. They stand
approximately 12in high and
are fully jointed. Kilbarchan, in
Scotland, where the artist
lives, is renowned as a
weaving village. While the
weavers worked in the
weaving shed, the children
would play with the bobbins
to keep themselves occupied.
These little bears are a
reminder of the "Weaver's
children from Kilbarchan."

SCENES

Single, pairs, or groups of Teddy Bears, usually dressed, and in a setting made up from suitable props, acquire a personality of their own. Scenes allow the artist the freedom to interpret the relationships of the bears through many fascinating arrangements, making them seem even more human.

▼ PAWS TOGETHER—EYES CLOSED
Linda Edwards of Little Treasures
Paws together is a 10in bear, saying her prayers by a handmade bed with antique bed linen. The bear is made of German mohair, glass eyes, suede pads, and is partly filled with pellets.

▲ TERRY AND HIS CHIMP
Vanessa Littleboy of Heritage Bears
Terry is a dressed 10in-tall mohair bear, with "flexilimbs" in the arms, glass eyes, and filled with polyester and pellets. The chimp is made in artificial silk and jointed. The artist says that children are very attracted to the antics of chimps so she chose to give one to her bear.

▶ THE ORGAN GRINDER
Janet Clarke of Teddystyle
This is a magnificent bear
standing 25in tall, made of
alpaca and mohair, with an
airbrushed face, shoe-button
eyes, "flexilimb" joints, and
tailored clothes. His monkey
is 12in tall, made of brown
and black tipped mohair, with
a felt face, hands, and feet,
flexible joints, and a felt
jacket and fez. They are
accompanied by their very
own handmade organ.

▲ THREE ONE-OF-A-KIND
BEARS
**Jenny Sharman-Cox of
Mister Bear**
This is a particularly charming
arrangement of three bears.
Their old fashioned clothes
and props (bag, boat,
umbrella), combined with their
antique look and particularly
the worn look of their noses,
work well together.

◀ THE BEAR-MAKER
**Sandie Goulder of
House of Bears**
This appealing bear stands
behind his wooden bench
with glue pot and tools,
working on a small bear that
he seems to be stuffing with
wood wool. His apron and
glasses give him a very
professional look.

GLUE

FANTASY BEARS

When creativity and imagination are allowed to roam free we can achieve extraordinary things. Bears are no exception. Taking flight from a story, a character, or a subject, and playing with fabrics, fur, cardboard, dyes, paint, and props, amazing things can develop. The bears can be as simple or as elaborate as your subject suggests. Let your imagination guide you and don't hold back your creativity.

▼ MACKINTOSH BEAR
Margaret Mcleen and Christine Gribbin of Growlies of Scotland

This 12in bear, made of short pile white mohair, with white Ultrasuede pads and black glass eyes, is named after the famous Scottish architect Charles Rennie Mackintosh. His unusual nose is based on a Mackintosh design and is made of four individual squares. The cravat is made with hand painted silk, again with a Mackintosh-style design on it, following his popular Rose theme.

▲ ONE BEAR AND ONE DALMATIAN
Jo Greeno

This gorgeous 22in bear is made in very long airbrushed mohair. It has "flexilimbs" on all limbs. The clothing, also made by the artist, is a dress and a coat with a long train, both made from animal-printed crushed velvet. The bear wears children's shoes and a hat. The gloves are made of felt with cardboard, and the false nails are painted with nail polish. She is holding a cigarette holder with cigarette.

The dog is made from crushed velvet, with joints in the head, gussets in the body, and is also airbrushed.

▶ GANDALF AND HELPERS
Diana Oldacre of Oldacre Bears

Gandalf, the Wizard, an imposing 26in, one-of-a-kind creation, is shown together with a group of his many-hued helpers, collecting magic pebbles to keep in their silver spell pots. The mohair for these bears was hand-dyed in a variety of unusual colors, along with velvets for their paws and satins for their ruffled collars. Gandalf's outstretched arms show his wide-sleeved satin and velvet robe. The outstretched arm pose is made possible by the use of a special "Lock-Line" armature in his upper body.

◄ BEARIE ON EARTH
Dagmar Strunck of Barenhowle, Germany
Combining the artist's message with the art of bear making, "Bearie on Earth, The Pride of Creation," depicts the great stupidity of human beings who would blow up the Earth for only a small moment of personal luck. He carries a document stating his distress.

▼ PROFESSOR BEAR
Carol-Lynn Rössel Waugh of the U.S.A.
This is an original gold mohair bear with glass eyes and a pair of antique glasses. His clever look and the book and pen he is holding clearly reveal him as a most intelligent bear.

SPECIAL BEARS
Sometimes you see a bear, or a scene featuring bears, that appeals in a very special way. It is the message that counts in these scenes, that gives them their special appeal. We show a few of those here, and hope they will inspire you to develop your own very special bear or scene.

▼ RECYCLED SPACE BEAR
Helga Torfs from Humpy Dumpy Bears in Belgium
This is an amazingly dressed bear made in antique gold mohair, stuffed with polyester and pellets, with bent legs and black glass eyes. All the accessories are made of recycled materials. The bear sits on the bear-planet looking at the pollution on Earth. He keeps his planet clean.

▲ THE SPIRIT OF CHRISTMAS
Penny Chalmers of Little Charmers
This piece was made specially for a Christie's sale of bears to benefit a children's home in Romania. It depicts the Romanian tradition where children put out their shoes for Saint Nicholas at Christmas. The 24in bear, with its magnificent velvet cloak representing the Saint, looks down on the two orphans.

MINIATURE BEARS

Miniature bears are currently very popular with makers and collectors, but in fact they have been made ever since the first Teddies appeared, early this century. Bears are considered miniatures if they are 5in or less in height, but many artists prefer to make them below 3in. The important thing is that they should be well proportioned, a scaled-down version of a larger bear. They can be made in short mohair pile or in velvety upholstery fabrics. They require special techniques but the final result is always most satisfying. Some are amazingly costumed, and sometimes they are arranged in scenes.

▼ SALUTE TO OLD PUNCH
Deborah Canham

Made by the pioneer of contemporary miniature bear making, this scene was inspired by traditional English puppets. It is set in a wooden theater with red and white striped tenting dyed to look old. The bears are made of mohair and Punch and Judy measure 4in each. The Baby measures 2in. The characters are constructed in a similar fashion to the original puppets, with weighted heads and Punch backs. They are costumed in silk, lawns, and antique laces. Punch and Judy have worn foot pads, and Baby's christening robe has a darn on the original lace panel.

◄ FAIRY BEAR
Elaine Lonsdale of Companion Bears

Fairy Bear is a 3½in miniature from the artist's collection of "Fairy Bears." It has been hand-sewn with a mohair head but a body made from cotton fabrics. He has cotter pin joints, Kapok and wood wool stuffing, and is weighted with a leather pouch full of steel shot which is fitted inside his stomach. His nose is stitched in antique embroidery silks, and he has silk flowers around his neck that are hand painted with fabric paints. On his head there is a tiny velvet bee alighting on a flower.

▼ BALLERINA AND CLOWN
Anne-Marie Wright of Plum Tree Bears

These miniature bears are dressed in elaborate costumes. The Clown costume is cleverly achieved by using upholstery velvet in different colors for the body, before adding ruffles, a hat, and a red nose. Ballerina's pink nose matches her dancing slippers.

◄ BLINKEY THE PIRATE
Elizabeth Leggat of Beth's Bears

This is one of the artist's old-style Teddy Bears with hump backs, long limbs, and shoe button type eyes. They are made from hand-dyed, specially treated mohair, giving them a "well-loved" look. They are fully jointed with steel washers and cotter pins and are entirely hand stitched. All the fabrics used for dressing are antique and vintage silks.

▲ THE CHIMNEY SWEEPS
Paula Strethill-Smith of Schultz Miniature Bears

These bears are made in hand-dyed distressed mohair plush. Smudger is a 4in bear wearing sack pants with belt and suspenders. Alfie sits in his cart with his tools, wearing street urchin pants tied with string, and a jaunty cap. The cart is pulled by Spike, a 3in terrier dog.

► LITTLE BROWN BEAR AND LITTLE GOLDEN GIRL
Pebby Morton of Pebby's Miniatures and the Tedi Bach Hug miniature bears' club

These 3in bears were made in upholstery fabric with Ultrasuede pads, jointed with cotter pin joints, with onyx beads for eyes. The girl bear is stuffed with polyfill, and dressed in a green gingham dress trimmed with narrow cotton lace. The boy bear is filled with a mixture of polyfill and steel shot, to make it heavier, and is dressed in pants and neckerchief, both made from fine polyester check fabric. The bears' clothing is hand-sewn.

▲ ERNEST
Iris and Ches Chesney of H. M. Bears

Ernest is a miniature replica of a 1903 18in tall German bear. He is made in mohair, fully jointed, with a wobbly head, specially loosened to look well worn, using a double cotter pin joint. He has ¼in glass eyes, and, unusually, was first hand-sewn and then machine stitched for increased strength.

Patterns—Mix and Match

Although this is a technical book rather than a project book, we are supplying three different bear patterns plus one miniature bear pattern for you to start practicing your bearmaking skills.

The patterns given in this section have been designed by the two authors and their two collaborators. The three main patterns will each produce a bear approximately 12½in high. The fourth pattern is a separate one, for a miniature bear. Bears made from these patterns have been used to illustrate the techniques explained in the book.

Each of the three larger patterns offers variations on the shape of the bear's body and limbs. You can choose from three different types of bodies, three types of arms, and three different leg shapes. Each head has its own distinctive shape.

These three bears can be made up either as they are, using all the parts designed by each artist to go together, or you can experiment by mixing and matching the patterns to obtain different effects for your bears: longer or shorter arms and legs, smaller or larger head, rounder or straighter body, etc.

However, there are a few items that should be kept together rather than mixed. They are:

1. Each head should match its corresponding head gusset.
2. Each arm should match its corresponding paw pad.
3. Each leg should match its corresponding footpad.

Bearing these in mind, you can experiment freely, combining heads, bodies, arms, legs, and ears in whichever way you like, and practice the techniques taught in the book until you are quite competent and feel you can start designing your own bears.

Seam allowances are included in all the patterns.

PATTERN A - Designed by Ann Stephens

This pattern, for a traditional-looking bear, has a wide head gusset, large feet, and looks good made in old-fashioned sparse mohair. Different noses, and differently placed ears, may make bears made from the same pattern look different.

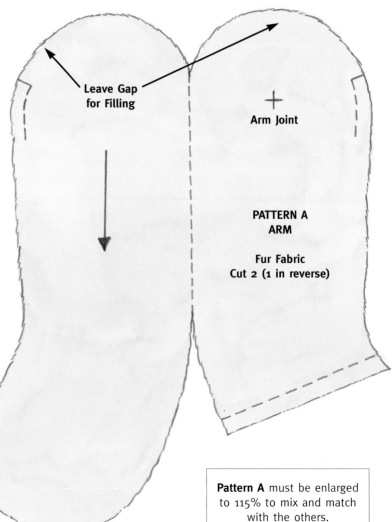

Leave Gap for Filling

Arm Joint

PATTERN A ARM

Fur Fabric
Cut 2 (1 in reverse)

Pattern A must be enlarged to 115% to mix and match with the others.

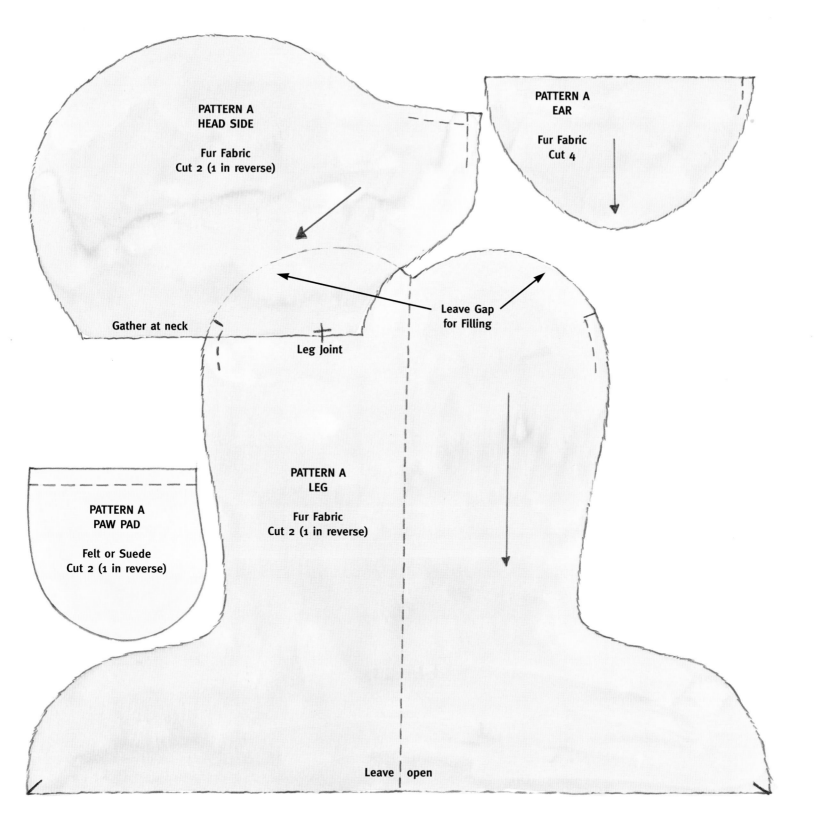

PATTERN A
HEAD SIDE

Fur Fabric
Cut 2 (1 in reverse)

PATTERN A
EAR

Fur Fabric
Cut 4

Gather at neck

Leg Joint

Leave Gap
for Filling

PATTERN A
LEG

Fur Fabric
Cut 2 (1 in reverse)

PATTERN A
PAW PAD

Felt or Suede
Cut 2 (1 in reverse)

Leave open

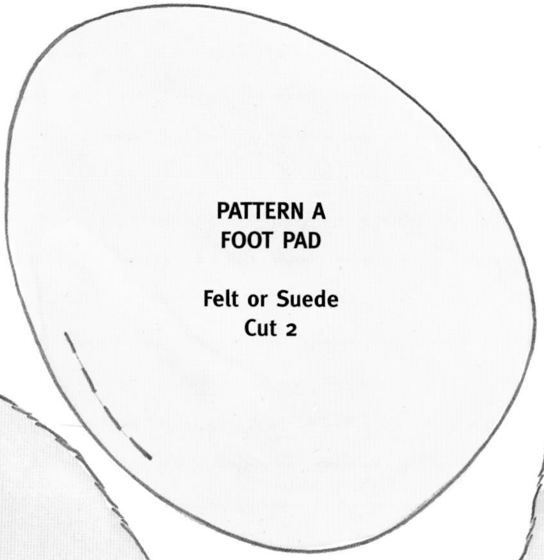

PATTERN A
FOOT PAD

Felt or Suede
Cut 2

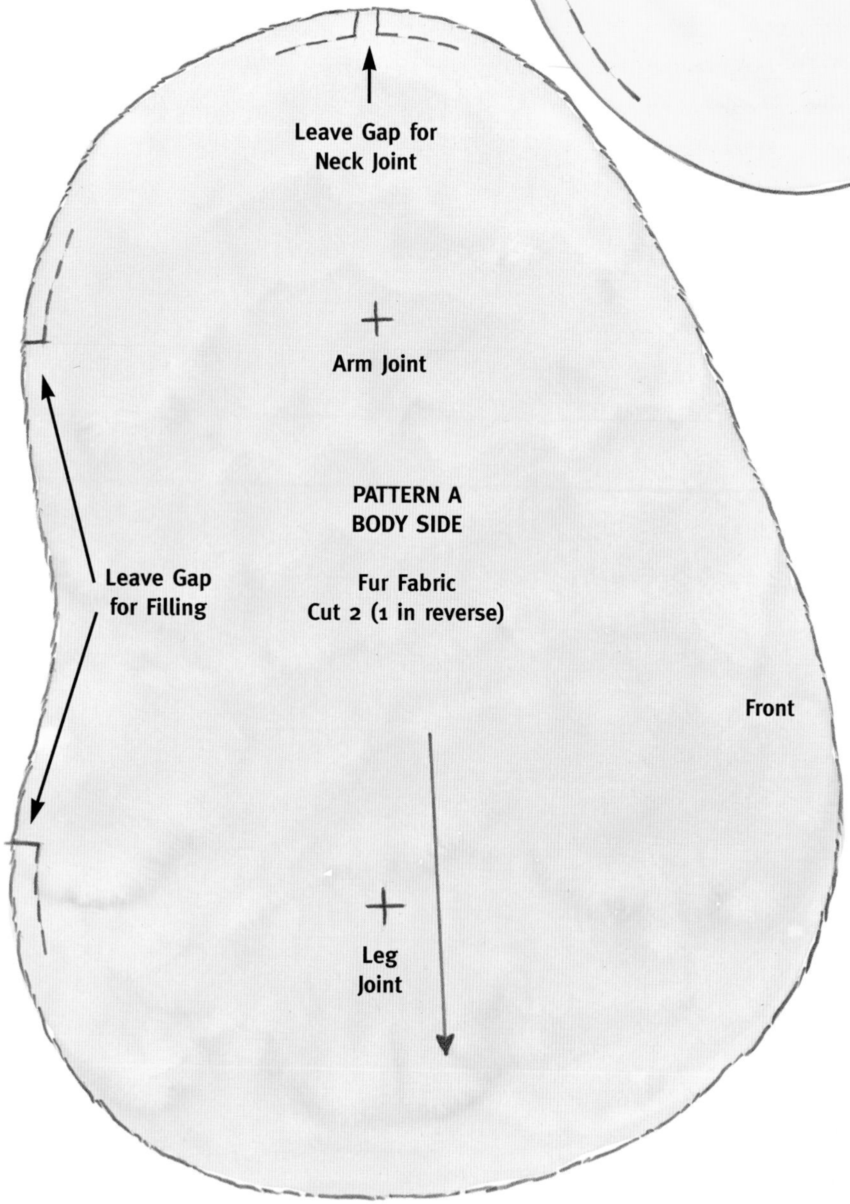

Leave Gap for
Neck Joint

Nose

+
Arm Joint

PATTERN A
HEAD GUSSET

Fur Fabric
Cut 1

PATTERN A
BODY SIDE

Fur Fabric
Cut 2 (1 in reverse)

Leave Gap
for Filling

Front

+
Leg
Joint

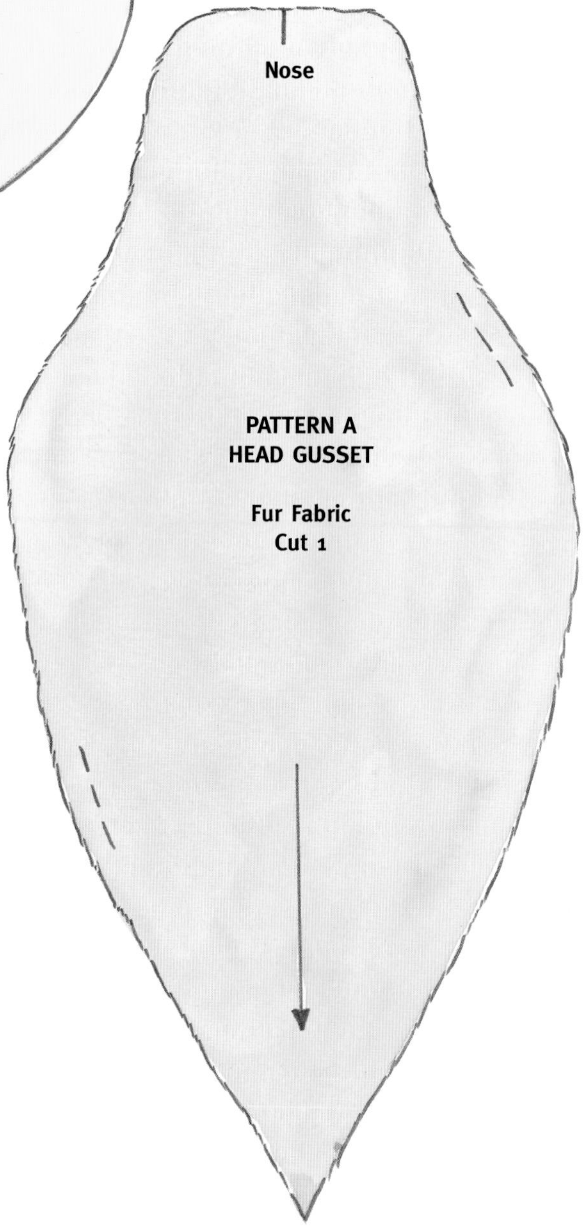

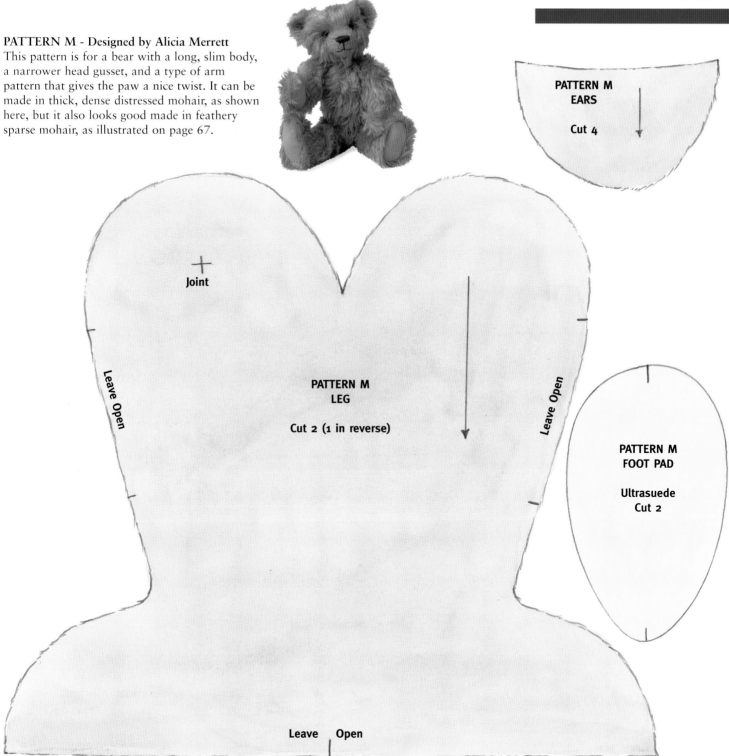

PATTERN M - Designed by Alicia Merrett
This pattern is for a bear with a long, slim body, a narrower head gusset, and a type of arm pattern that gives the paw a nice twist. It can be made in thick, dense distressed mohair, as shown here, but it also looks good made in feathery sparse mohair, as illustrated on page 67.

PATTERN M
EARS

Cut 4

Joint

Leave Open

PATTERN M
LEG

Cut 2 (1 in reverse)

Leave Open

PATTERN M
FOOT PAD

Ultrasuede
Cut 2

Leave Open

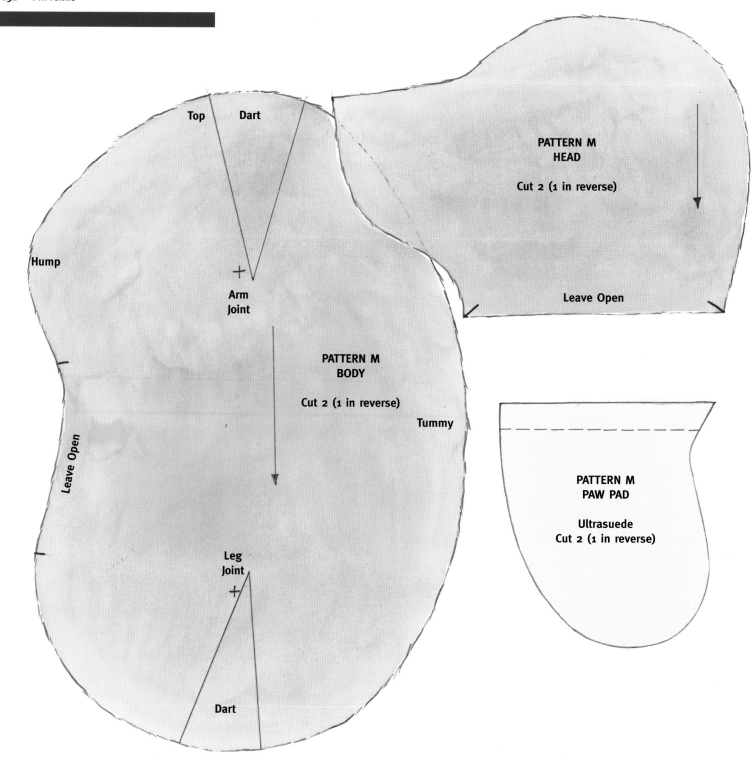

Top Dart

Hump

Arm
Joint

Leave Open

PATTERN M
BODY

Cut 2 (1 in reverse)

Tummy

Leg
Joint

Dart

PATTERN M
HEAD

Cut 2 (1 in reverse)

Leave Open

PATTERN M
PAW PAD

Ultrasuede
Cut 2 (1 in reverse)

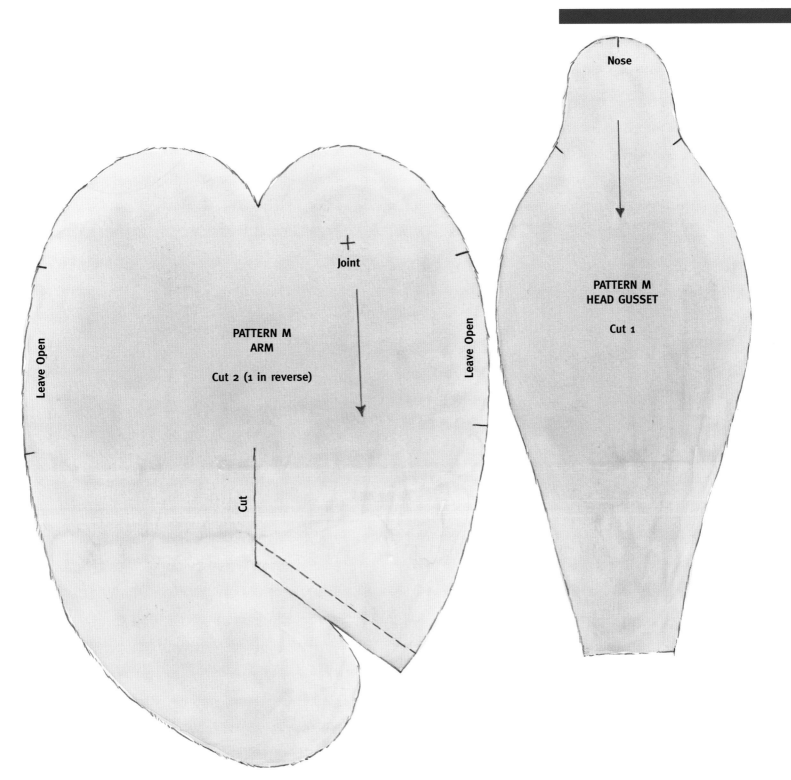

Nose

PATTERN M
HEAD GUSSET

Cut 1

+
Joint

PATTERN M
ARM

Cut 2 (1 in reverse)

Leave Open

Leave Open

Cut

PATTERN D - Designed by Diana Oldacre
The original pattern for all the dressed bears in the Garments section, this is a modern bear, with a shorter body, a round head with a high brow, and arms and legs constructed from separate outer and inner patterns. It looks good made in short and dense mohair, or in a thick, long, and curly fur.

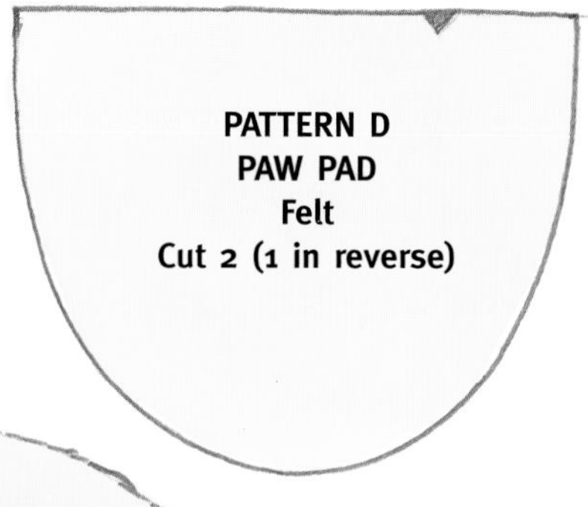

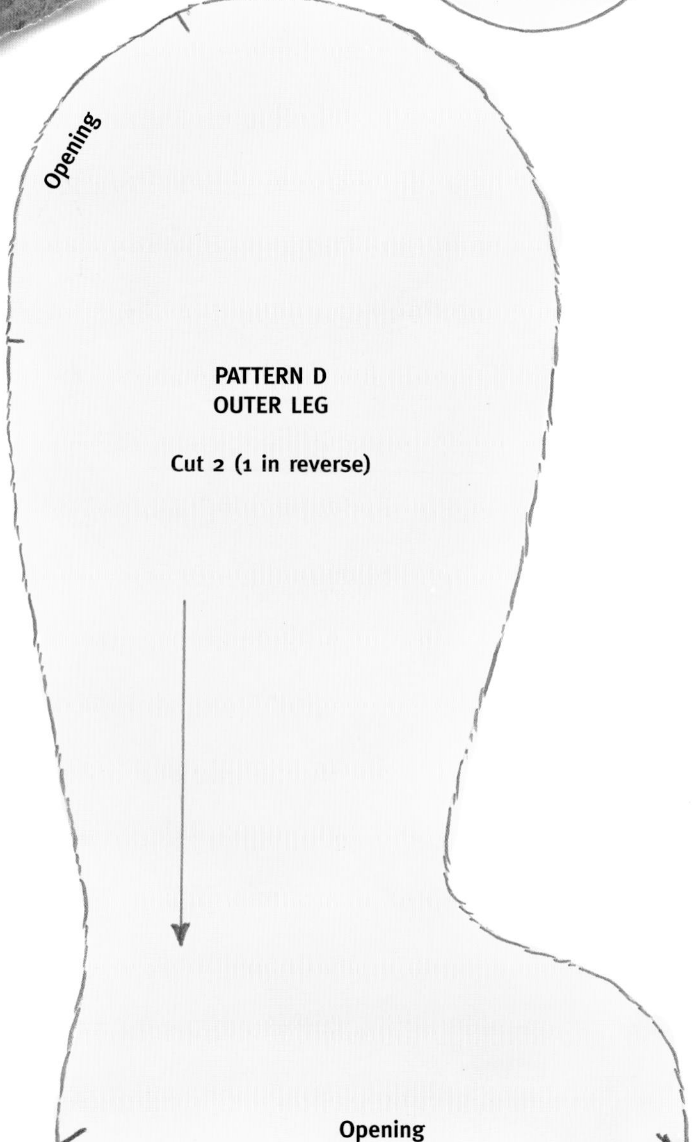

PATTERN D
PAW PAD
Felt
Cut 2 (1 in reverse)

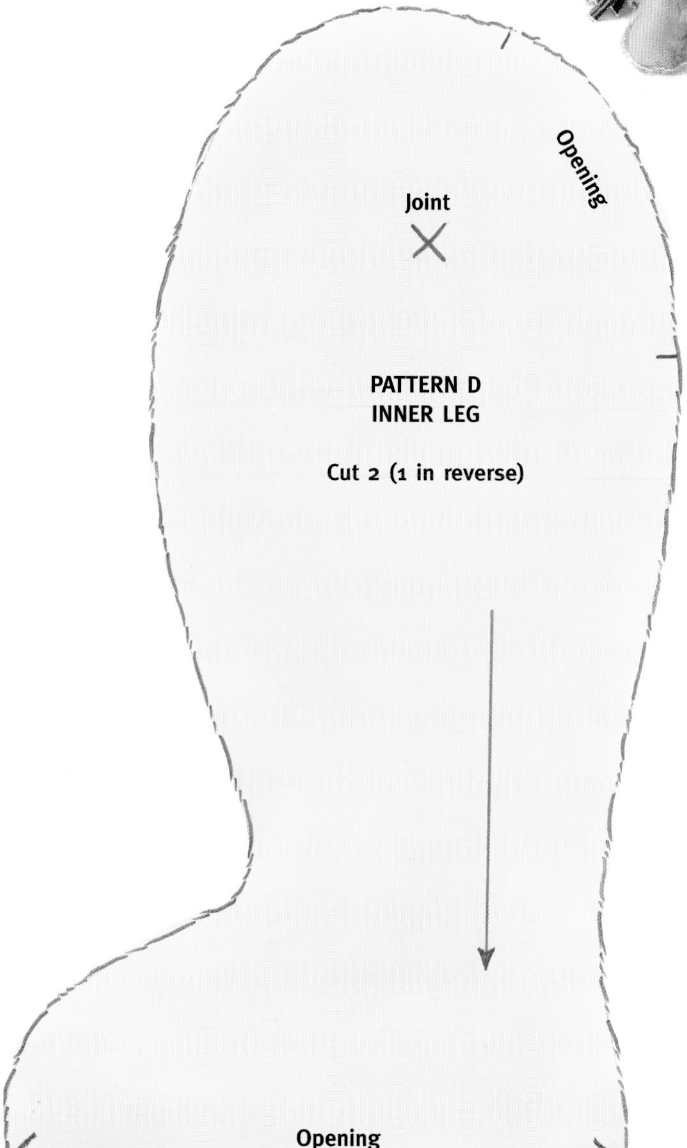

Joint

Opening

PATTERN D
INNER LEG

Cut 2 (1 in reverse)

Opening

PATTERN D
OUTER LEG

Cut 2 (1 in reverse)

Opening

Opening

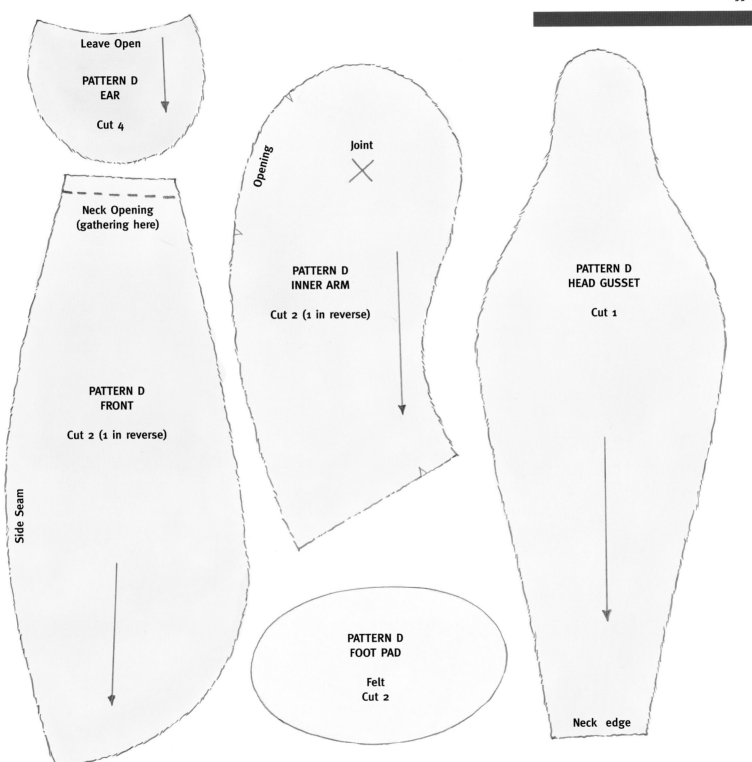

Leave Open

PATTERN D
EAR

Cut 4

Neck Opening
(gathering here)

PATTERN D
FRONT

Cut 2 (1 in reverse)

Side Seam

Opening

Joint

PATTERN D
INNER ARM

Cut 2 (1 in reverse)

PATTERN D
HEAD GUSSET

Cut 1

PATTERN D
FOOT PAD

Felt
Cut 2

Neck edge

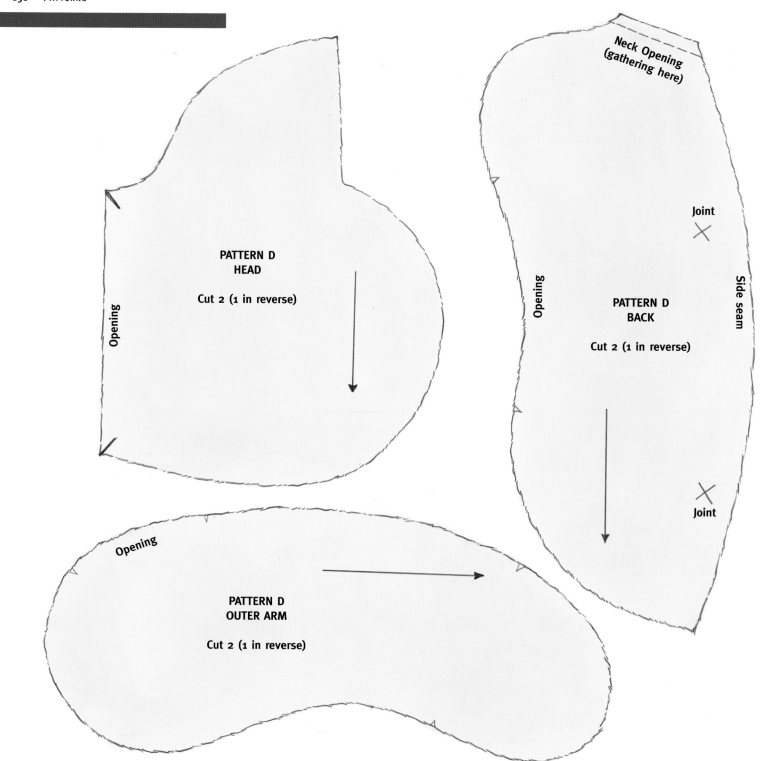

**PATTERN D
HEAD**

Cut 2 (1 in reverse)

Opening

**Neck Opening
(gathering here)**

Joint

Opening

**PATTERN D
BACK**

Cut 2 (1 in reverse)

Side seam

Joint

Opening

**PATTERN D
OUTER ARM**

Cut 2 (1 in reverse)

MINIATURE BEAR PATTERN - designed by Pebby Morton

A nice, easy pattern for a first attempt at making a miniature bear. It has a body with a hump at the back, long arms, and a well-shaped head. Upholstery fabric is recommended for beginners. The vest can be made in felt or Ultrasuede.

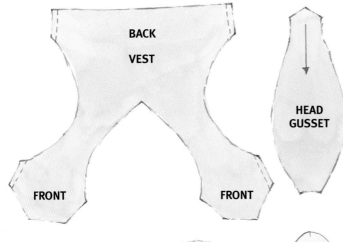

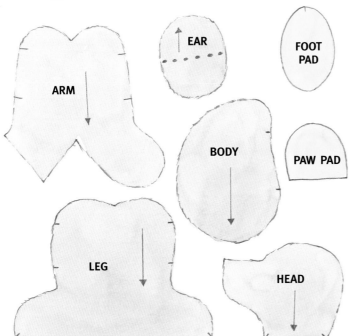

International Mail-Order Suppliers

EDINBURGH IMPORTS INC
POB 340, Newbury Park
CA 91319-0340
USA
Tel/Fax: (805) 376 1700/1711

Everything for Teddy Bears; quality craft suppliers since 1981.

SPARE BEAR PARTS
Box 56F Interlochen
MI 49643
USA
Tel: (616) 276 7915
Fax: (616) 276 7921

Bear makers' suppliers; everything for quality teddies.

CHRISTIE BEARS
92 The Green, Kings Norton, Birmingham B38 8RS, U.K.
Tel/fax: 0121 459 8817
(From overseas: 011 44 121 459 8817)
E-mail: christiebs@aol.com
(for inquiries only)

Leading specialist in materials and components for traditional collectors' bears.

OAKLEY FABRICS LTD.
8 May Street, Luton, Beds.
LU1 3QY, U.K.
Tel: 01582 734733/424828

Fax: 01582 455274
(From overseas: 011 44 1582 734733 or 455274)

Europe's largest stockist of mohair and bearmaking components.

TEDI BACH HUG
c/o 1 Blandford Road,
Ipswich, Suffolk
IP3 8SL, U.K.

Miniature Bear Club. Suppliers of fabrics, components, and kits for miniature bears only.

Sources of Information on Bear Fairs, Bear Artists and Suppliers

TEDDY BEAR AND FRIENDS
The complete magazine for Teddy Bear lovers. Published by Cumberland Publishing Inc, 6405 Flank Drive, Harrisburg, PA 17112, USA

THE UK TEDDY BEAR GUIDE
The essential resource for all Teddy Bear lovers. Published by Hugglets, PO Box 290, Brighton BN2 1DR, U.K.

Index

A

all fours, bears on 128–29
antiquing 82, 86–7
appeal, special, bears 144–5
arms 24, 25, 40
awls 12

B

backstitch 19
beads, glass 58
bells 9
bloomers 110
bodies 24, 33–5
bow ties 103
brushes, teasel 12

C

caps 101, 106–7
children's bears 9, 49, 58
classic bears 122–28
claws, embroidered 84
closing openings 59
clothes
  making 100–17
  simple 132–33
  stitching 19
  unusual 134–35
collars 101, 104, 108
collectors' bears
  fabric choice 30
  joints for 46, 48
  safety 8, 9
coloring bears 82, 83
colors of fabrics 14
components, safety 8, 9

costumes *see* clothes
cotter keys 12, 48
cotter pin joints 18, 48, 52, 56
  miniature bears 94, 96–7
cutting
  fabric 29, 30, 32
  practice patterns 100

D

darts 22, 33, 38
designing 22–7
distressing 86–7
documentation 9
dresses 101, 110
dungarees 101, 114–15

E

ears 80–1
  designing 27
  miniature bears 95
  stitching 39
embroidery
  claws and pads 84
  mouths 78–9
  noses 74–5, 77, 94
  threads 10
enlarging patterns 28, 100
equipment 10–13
eyes 17, 66–71
  miniature bears 95
  placement 29
  points in designing 27
  safety 9, 66

F

fabrics 9, 14–15, 36
  backings for glass eyes 70
  clothes 100

cutting 29, 30, 32
marking for joints 52–3
miniature bears 90
painting 83
patterns, placement
on/tracing onto 30
pile 29, 30–1
turning 52–3, 93
fantasy bears 142–3
features, special 130–31
filling see stuffing
flexible stems 16, 25, 55
footpads *see* paw pads
forceps 12, 53, 72–3, 93

G

garments *see* clothes
glass
  beads 58
  eyes 17, 66–70
growlers 9, 18, 62–3, 87
gussets, head 22, 26–7, 36–7

H

hats 101, 106–7
heads 24, 26–7, 36–8, 94–5
history
  bears 6
  eyes 66
homey bears 136–7

I

inserts, flexible 16, 25, 55
inspirations for bear-making
120–47

J

joint punches 12

joints 9, 18, 46–57
  miniature bears 94, 96–7
  placement in designs 29

K

kapok 16, 62
knickers, patterns 101

L

labels 8, 9
ladder stitch 19, 59
layout of fabric 30–1
leather noses 76
legs 24, 25, 42–3
limbs
  bendable 16, 25, 55
  designing 24, 25

M

machine stitching 19, 36
  see also stitching
marking fabric 30–1, 52–3
  tools 12
materials 9, 10, 14–18
miniature bears 14, 90–7,
146–7, 157
modern bears 25, 58, 154–6
mouths 78–9
musical
  movements 9, 18, 62, 63
  pushbuttons 18
'mutton chop' effect 73
muzzle, stuffing and trimming
72–3

N

nap of fabric 29, 30–1
neck joints, swivel 18, 50–1

needles 10
noses 18
　embroidery 74–5
　leather 76
　miniature bears 94
　safe 9, 77
　trimming 72–3
nut and bolt joints 18, 46–7, 52, 55
nut drivers 12, 46–7

O
observing bears 22–23
openings, closing 59

P
pads *see* paw pads
painting
　fabric 83
　glass eyes 70
pairs of bears 138–9
pants 101, 112
patterns 28–9
　bears 148–57
　clothes 100–1
　miniature bears 90, 157
　placement on/tracing onto fabric 30
paw pads
　designing 25
　embroidered 84
　fabric choice 14, 30
　finishing 82
　raised 85
　stitching 41, 43
　tracing and cutting 31
pellets, plastic 16, 60
pile of fabric 29, 30–1

pinning
　body 34
　fabrics 33, 36
pins 10
placement
　in designs, of eyes and joints 29
　of patterns on fabric 30, 31
plastic
　eyes 17, 66, 71
　joints 18, 49, 52
　noses 77
　pellets 16, 60
pliers 12
polyester stuffing 16, 58
positioning
　ears 80
　eyes 68
proportions of bears 22, 23, 24
　clothes-making 100
pushbuttons, musical 18

R
reproducing patterns 28, 100

S
safety 8–9
　eyes 17, 66, 71
　joints 18, 49, 52
　noses 77
satin stitch 19
scale, miniature bears 90
scalpels 12, 32
scarves 106
scenes 140–1
scissors 12, 32, 72
seam allowances 29, 90, 100

sewing *see* stitching
shaping bears 82–3
shirts 101, 116–17
shot, steel 16
skirts 108–9
soft-sculpting 82–3
spectacles 9, 18
stab stitch 19
stems, flexible 16, 25, 55
stitches 19, 59
stitching
　arms 40
　bodies 33–5
　clothes 100
　darts 38
　ears 39, 80–1
　eyes 68–9
　heads 36–8
　legs 42–3
　miniature bears 90–2, 94–5, 96–7
　mouths 78–9
　paw pads 41, 43
　threads 10, 33, 36, 59
stuffing and stuffings 16, 58–63
　miniature bears 94, 96–7
　sticks 12, 53, 58
suppliers 157
sweatshirts, patterns 101
swivel neck joints 18, 50–1

T
t-shirts 112
threads 10, 33, 36, 59
ties 103, 105
tools 10–13, 93
tracing

patterns onto fabric 30
shapes of bears 22–23
tracksuits 113
Trading Standards 8, 9
traditional bears 120–21
　history 6
　stuffing 58
traditional-looking bear pattern 148–50
trousers 101, 112
turning fabric 52–3, 93
tweezers 93

V
vests 100, 102, 108

W
waistcoats 100, 102, 108
wood wool 16, 61
wrenches, ratchet 12

Credits

Quarto Publishing would like to acknowledge and thank the following for providing pictures and for permission to reproduce copyright material. While every effort has been made to acknowledge copyright holders we would like to apologize should there have been any omissions.

Key: t = top, b = bottom, r = right, l = left, c = center

Barbara Ann Bears p.127(r); Atlantic Bears p.124(r); Barenhowle p.144(tl); Bear Paws Collectables p.129(tr); Beth's Bears p.147(tl); Bocs Teganau p.58(tl), 126(t); Brodie Bears p.130(b); Burlington Bearties p.130(tr); Deborah Canham p.146(l); Hilary Clark p.9(tl), 137(br); Cloth Ears p.28, 44/45, 64/65, 122; Companion Bears p.9(br), 146(tr); Cupboard Bears p.136(t); Dormouse Designs p.139(t); Enchanted Bears p.137(tr); Jo Greeno p.136(b), 142(tr); Gregory Bears p.129(b); Growlies p.142(bl); Hairy Beary Co. p.78(tl); Renate Hanisch p.137(l); F.J. Hannay p.1(l), 127(l); Hembury Bears p.128(l), 131(tr), 134(l); Heritage Bears p.140(tr); Anita Hill p.131(bl); H.M. Bears p.7(tl), 86(tl), 118, 120(bl), 147(r); House of Bears p.141(br); Humpy Dumpy Bears p.145(bl); Naomi Laight p.133(r); Little Charmers p.145(tr); Little Treasures p.13 (b), 140(bl); Norbeary Bears p.135(t); Malvern Bears p.132(l); Alicia Merrett p. 1(c/r), 2(l), 3(l), 8(l), 10, 30, 52(tl), 63, 73, 77, 79, 124(l), 151; Merrythought p.121(bl); Mister Bear p.133(l), 135(bl), 141(l); Mother Hubbard p.132(br); My Old Teddy p.132(tr); The Nostalgic Bear Co. p.128(r); Oldacre Bears p.3(r), 7(bl/tr), 14, 19, 98/99, 103, 105, 106, 107, 109, 111, 112, 113, 115, 117, 125, 143, 154; Old Bexley Bears p.123(l); Only Natural p.119(b), 123(r); Paula-Bears p.138(t); Sue Pearson Collection p.6(l), 36, 121(c/r); Pebby's Miniatures p.2(r), 97(br), 147(bl), 157; Louise Peers p.90(tl); Pictor p.22(br); Yvonne Plakké p.135(br); Plum Tree Bears p.88, 146(br); Carol-Lynn Rössel Waugh p.8(r), 22(tl), 46(tl), 82(tl), 100(tl), 119(t), 144(b); Schultz Miniature Bears p.147(tr); Something's Bruin p.126(r); Soulmate Bears p.130(tl); Ann Stephens p.2(c), 3(c), 6(r), 33, 51, 71, 75, 81, 87, 148(tr); Tedi Bach Hug Miniature Bears' Club p.147(bl); Teddystyle p.141(tr); Theodore's Bear Emporium p.134(tl); Sue Tolcher p.7(br); Waifs and Strays p.139(b); Wood-U-Like Bears p.129(t), 131(br). We are grateful for permission to reproduce pictures from the Christie's catalogue of December 1996.

All other photographs are copyright of Quarto Publishing plc.

Quarto would like to thank Diana Oldacre, of Oldacre Bears, for the Garments section; Pebby Morton, of Pebby's Miniatures, for the Miniature Bears section; and Juley Merrett for general help. We are also grateful to Oakley Fabrics and Christie Bears for supplying tools, equipment, and material for use in the book; and to Hugglets for all their help, and particularly for providing space for photography during their Teddies '97 Fair.